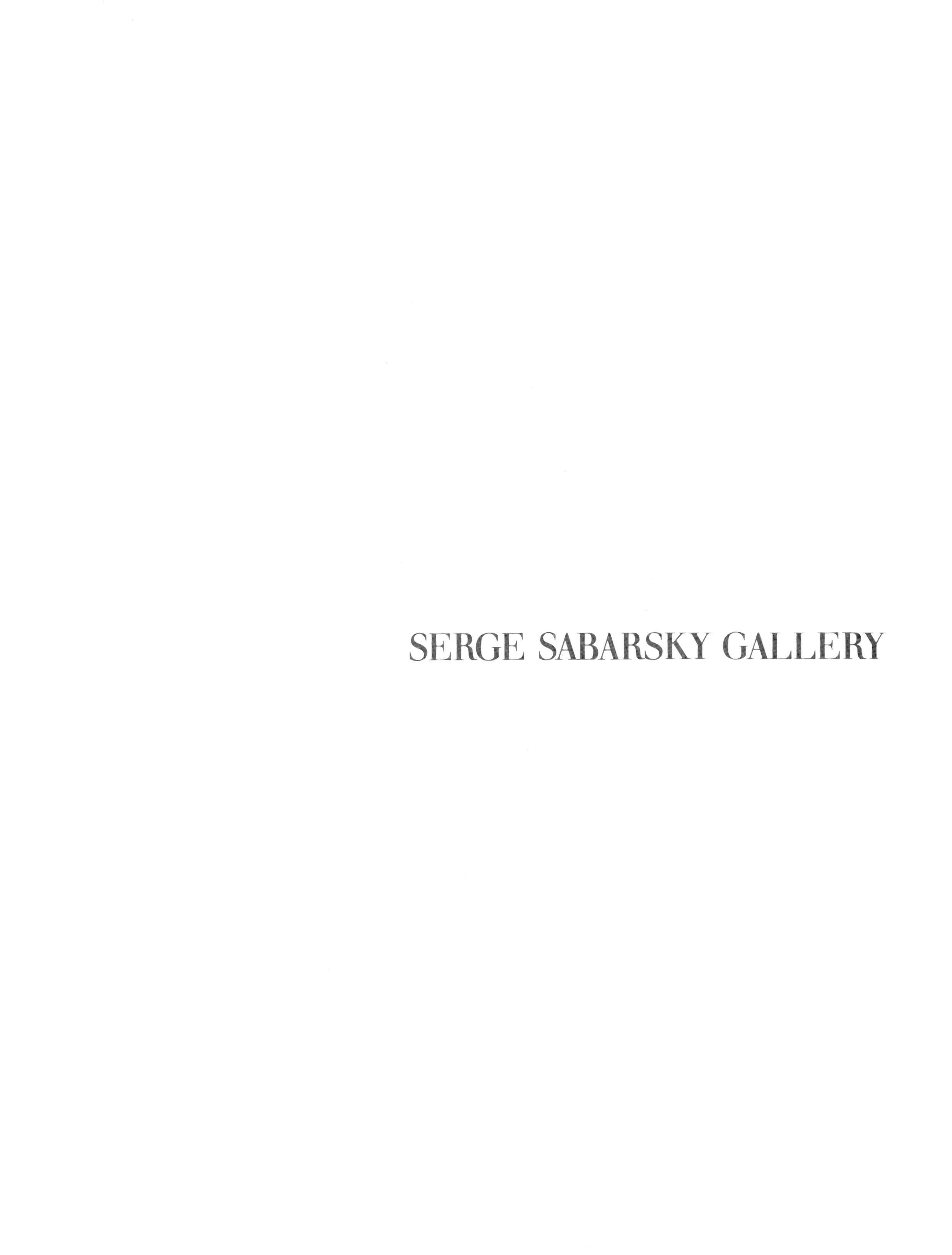
SERGE SABARSKY GALLERY

# expressionists

Major paintings, water-colors,
drawings and sculptures by
17 German Expressionists
at the
SERGE  SABARSKY  GALLERY

The works reproduced in this catalogue
are being shown in three consecutive
exhibitions at the

## SERGE SABARSKY GALLERY

987 MADISON AVENUE        NEW YORK, N.Y. 10021
PHONE: (212) 628-6281       CABLES: SERGALRY NEW YORK

All works are for sale; additional
information and prices on request.

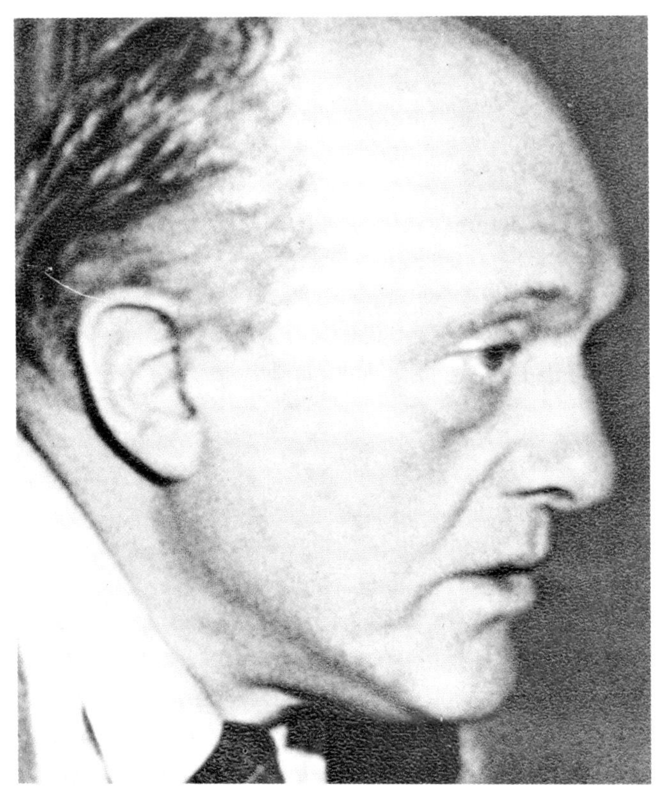

# Max Beckmann

LEIPZIG 1884 - 1950 NEW YORK

1  Portrait of Herr Pagel
Oil on canvas, 1907
36½ x 29″ (92.7 x 73.6 cm)
Signed and dated upper right:
Beckmann 07

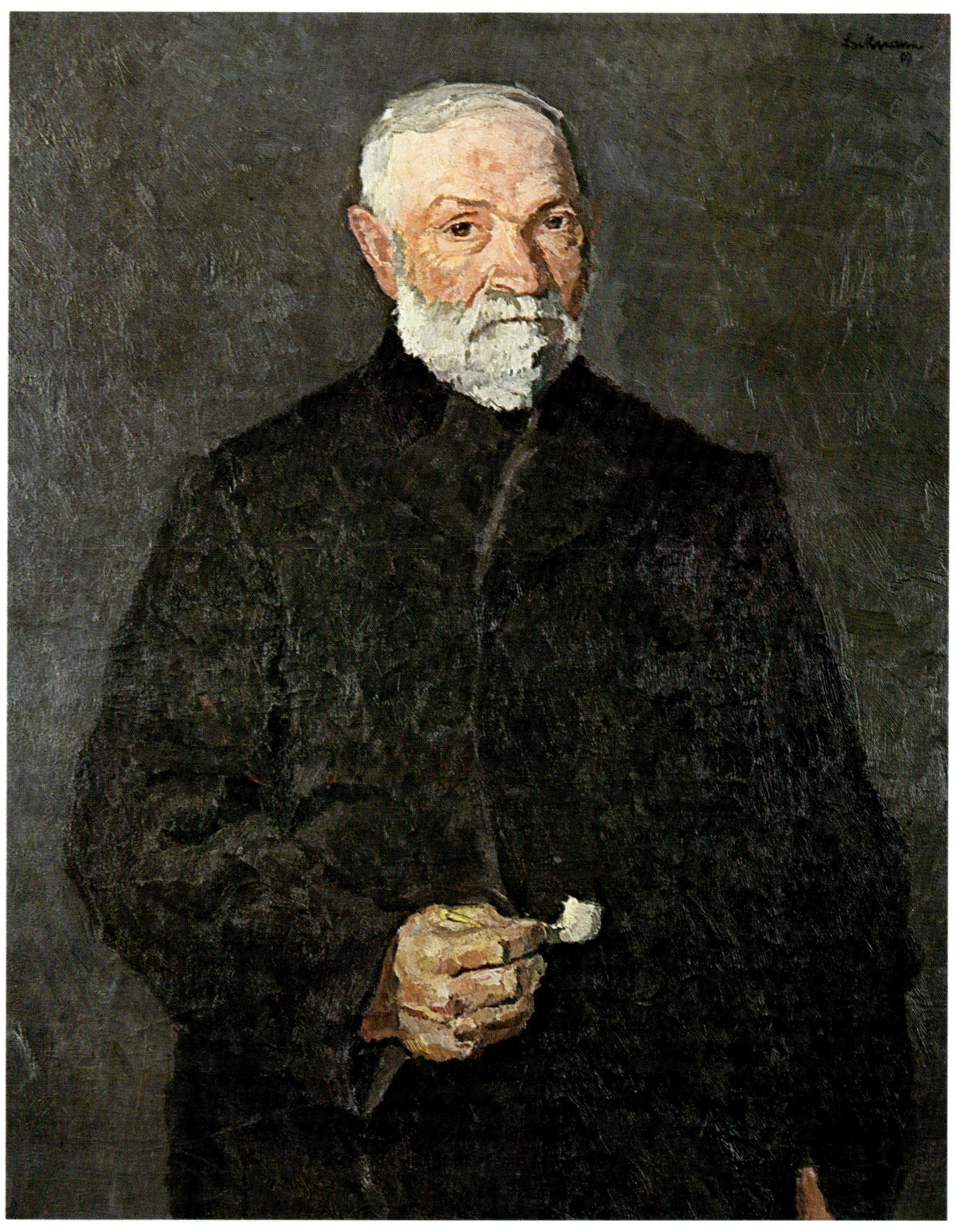

# Max Beckmann

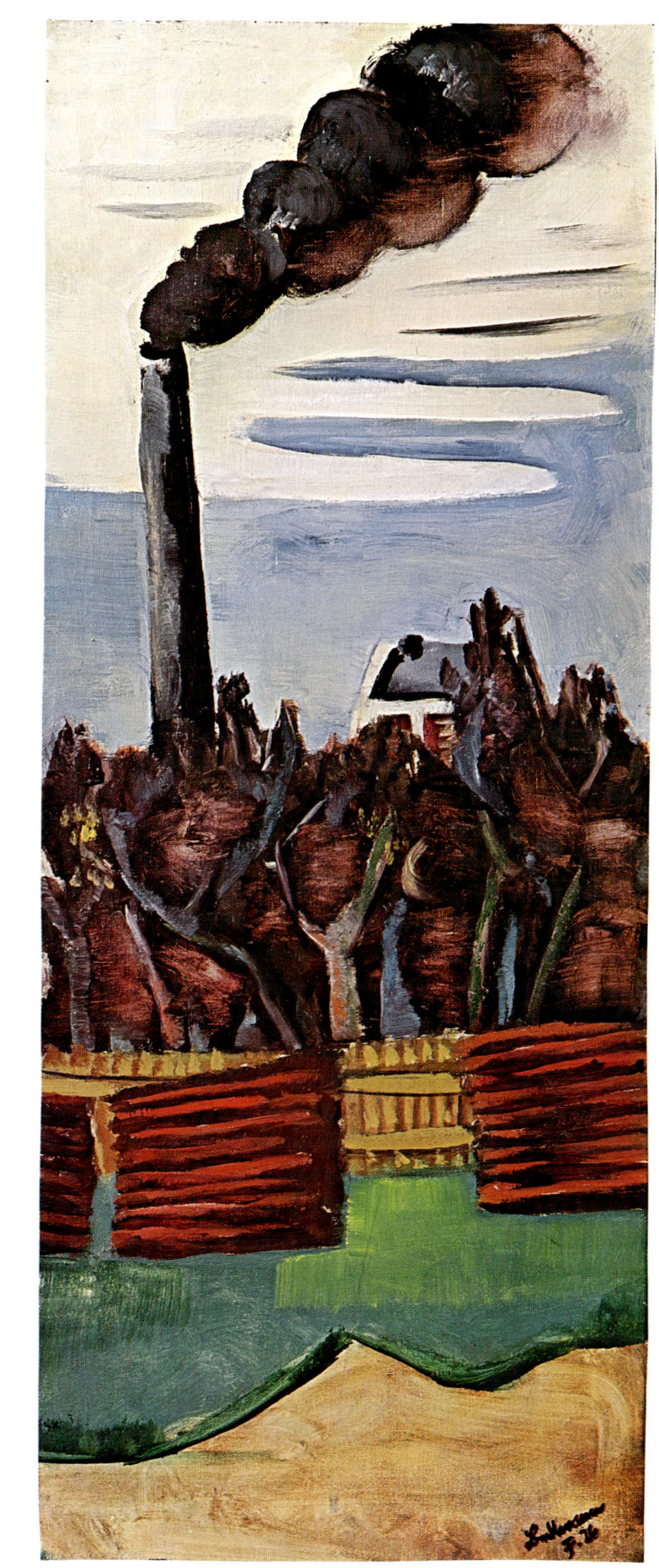

# Max Beckmann

3 Claridge II
Oil on canvas, 1930
35¼″ x 17¾″ (89.5 x 45 cm)

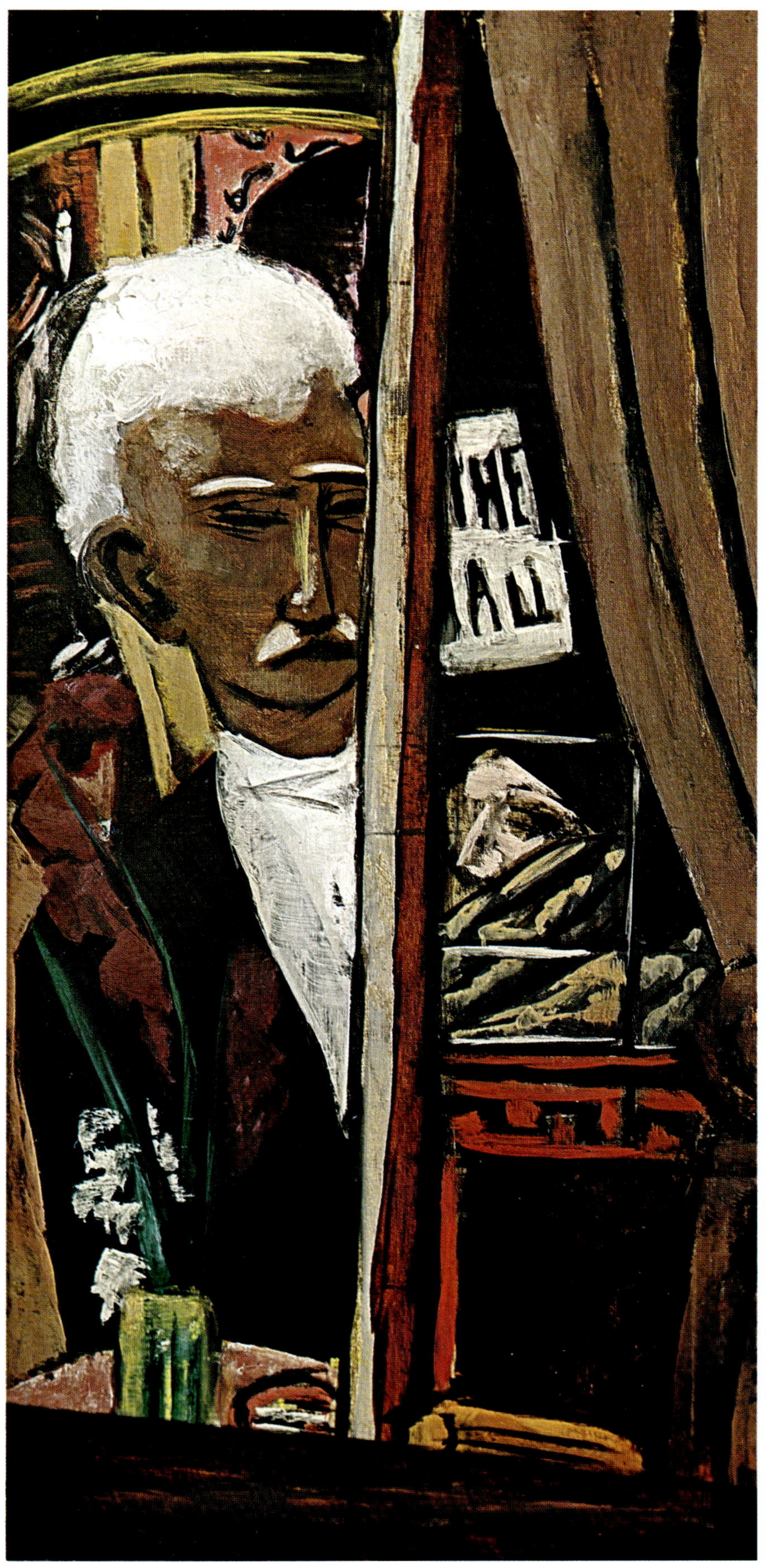

# Max Beckmann

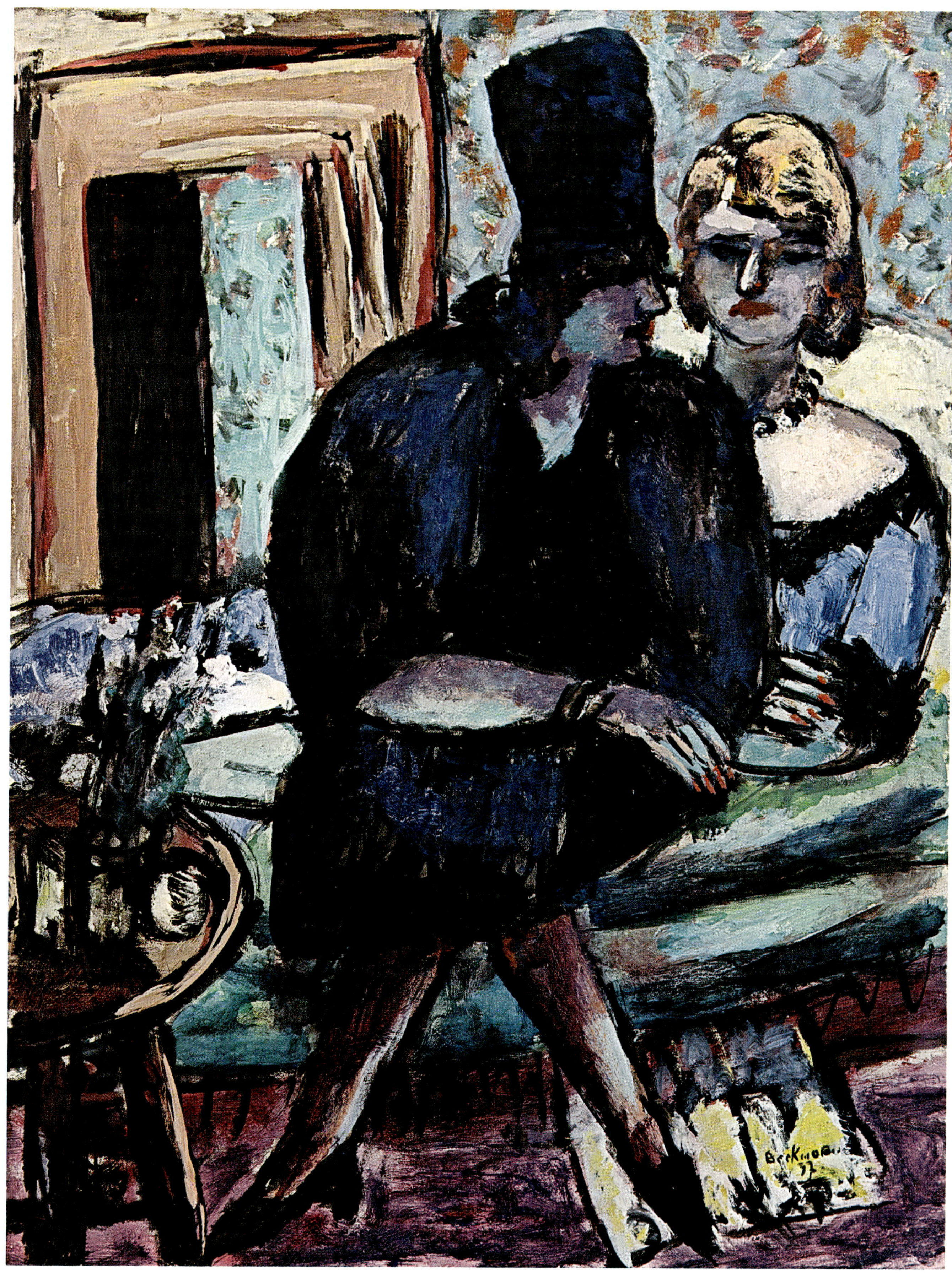

# Max Beckmann



Heisse Quellen bei Abano
*(Hot Springs at Abano)*
Oil on canvas, 1939
19¾ x 31¾″ (50.1 x 80.6 cm)
Signed and dated lower right:
Beckmann A.39 [Amsterdam 1939]

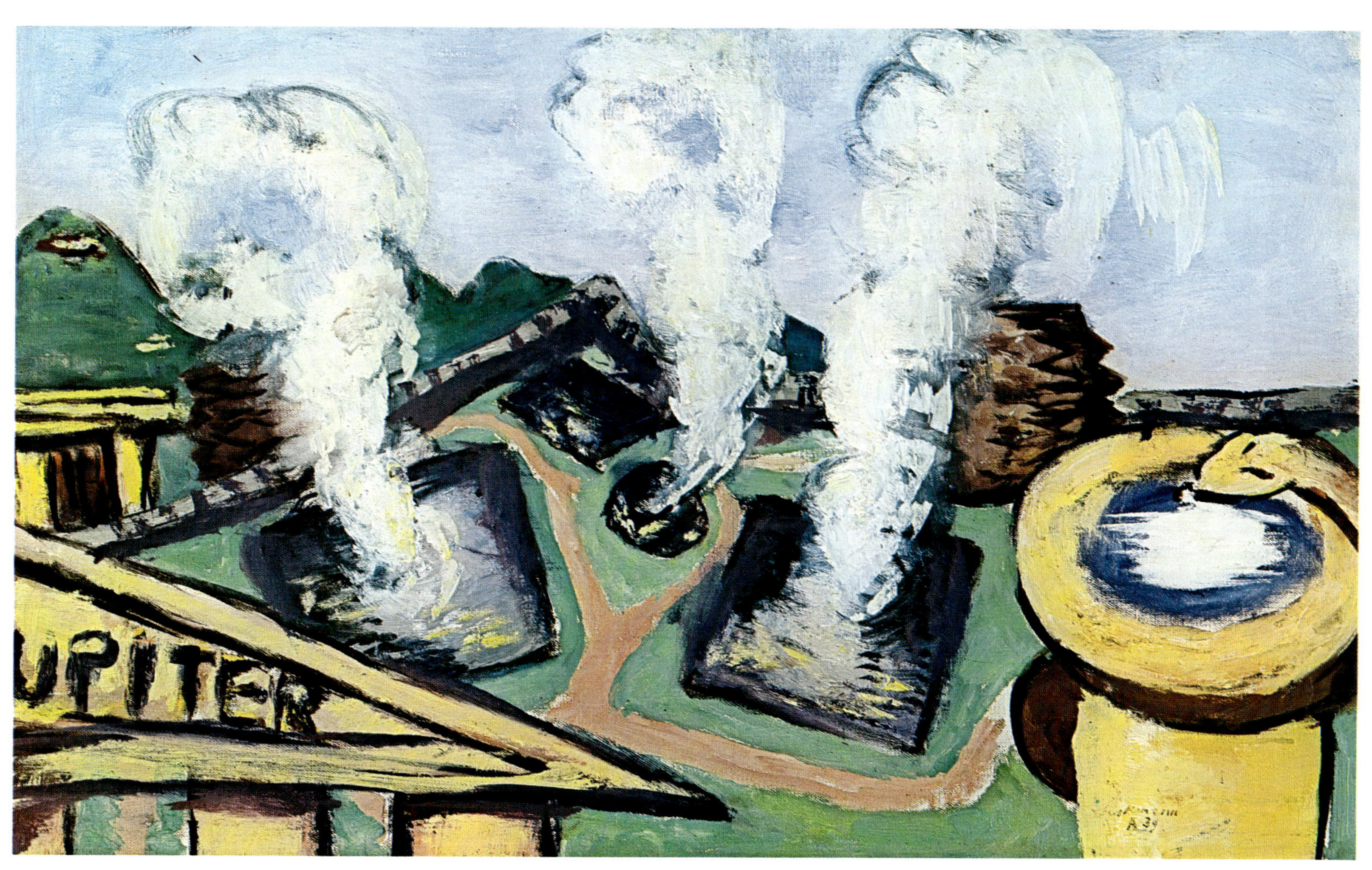
UPITER

Max Beckmann

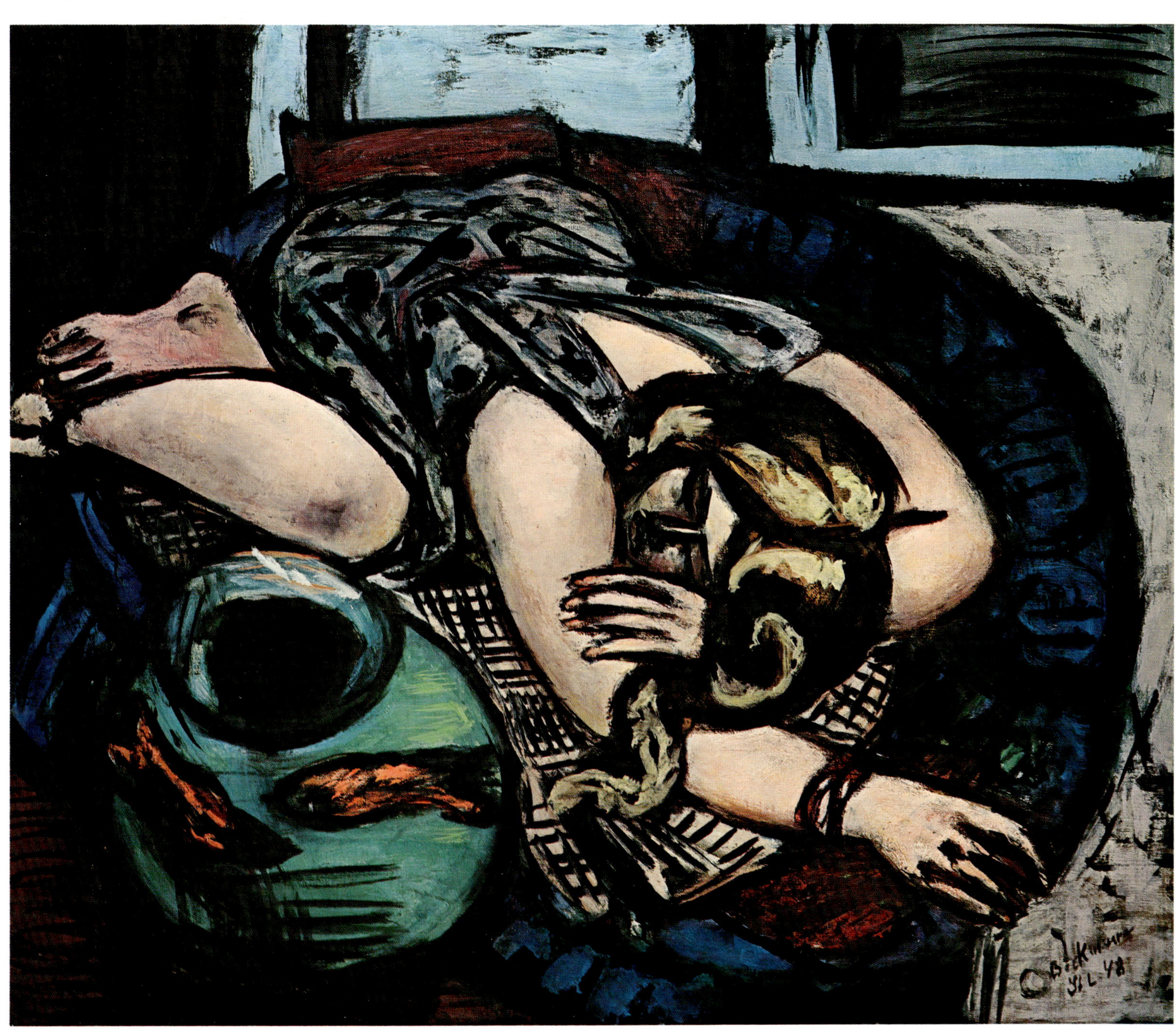

# Max Beckmann

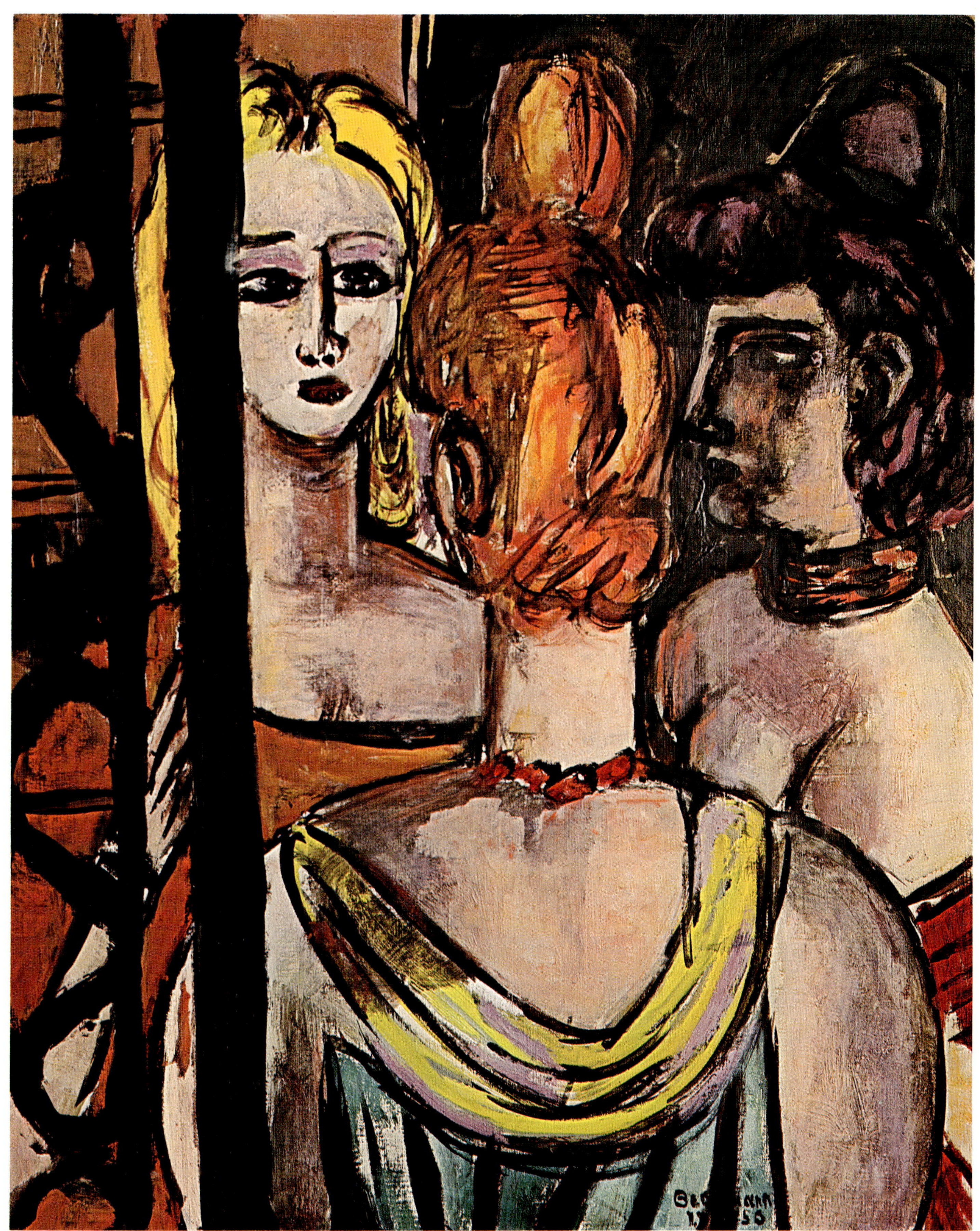

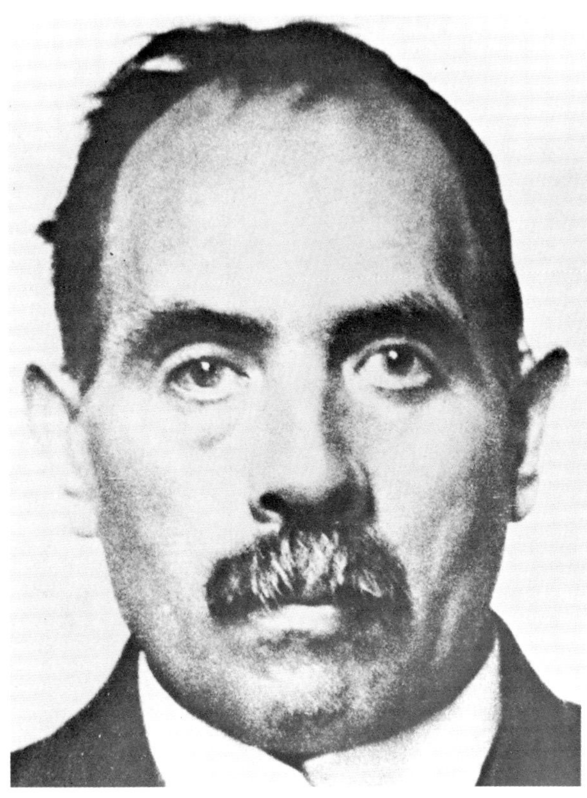

# Lovis Corinth

TAPIAU 1858 - 1925 ZANDVOORT

8 Red Roses
Oil on canvas, 1913
39⅜ x 31¾″ (100 x 80.6 cm)
Signed and dated center right

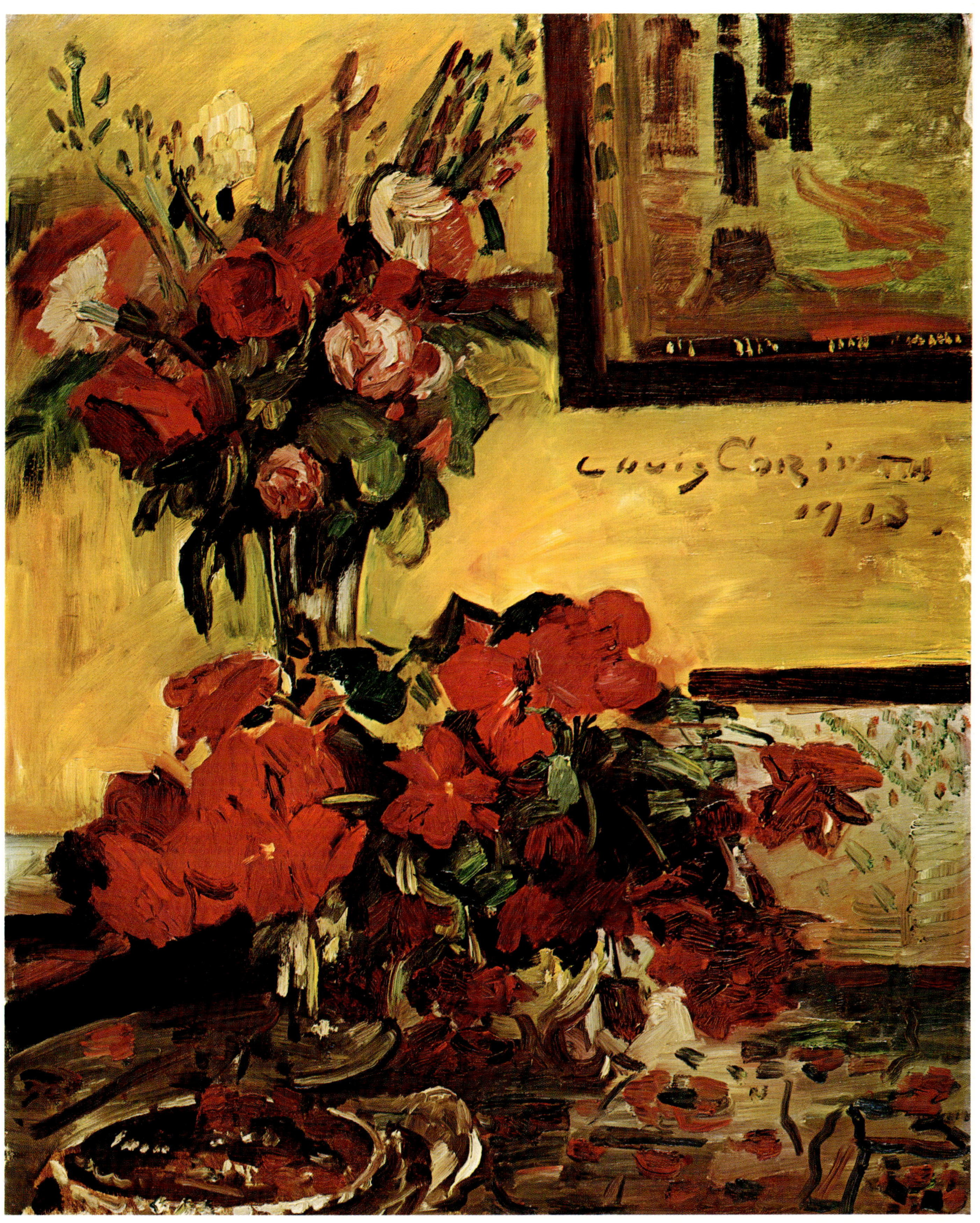

Louis Corinth
1913.

# Lovis Corinth

9   Walchensee Fountain
Oil on canvas, 1920
42½ x 31″ (108 x 78.7 cm)
Signed and dated lower left

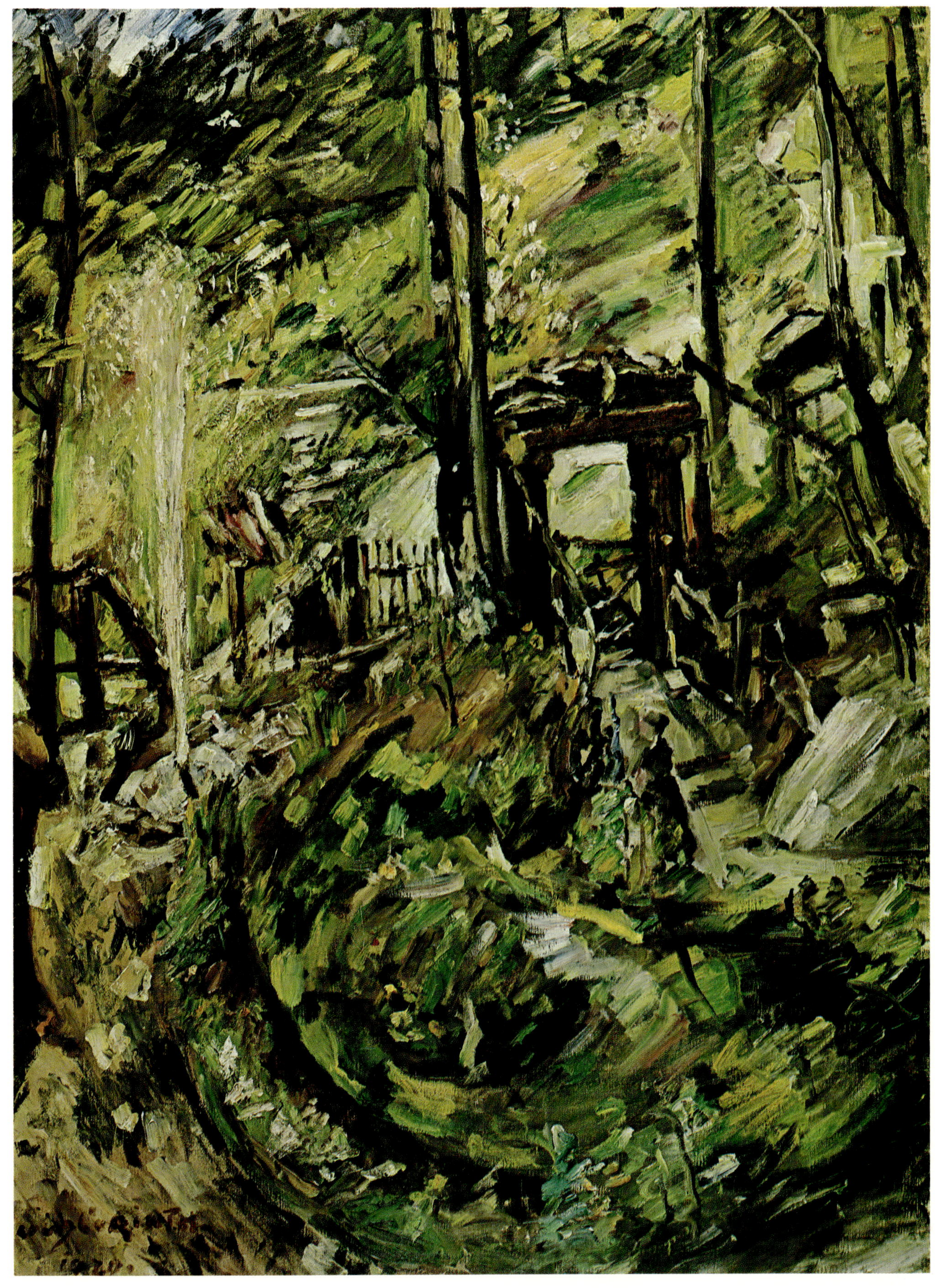

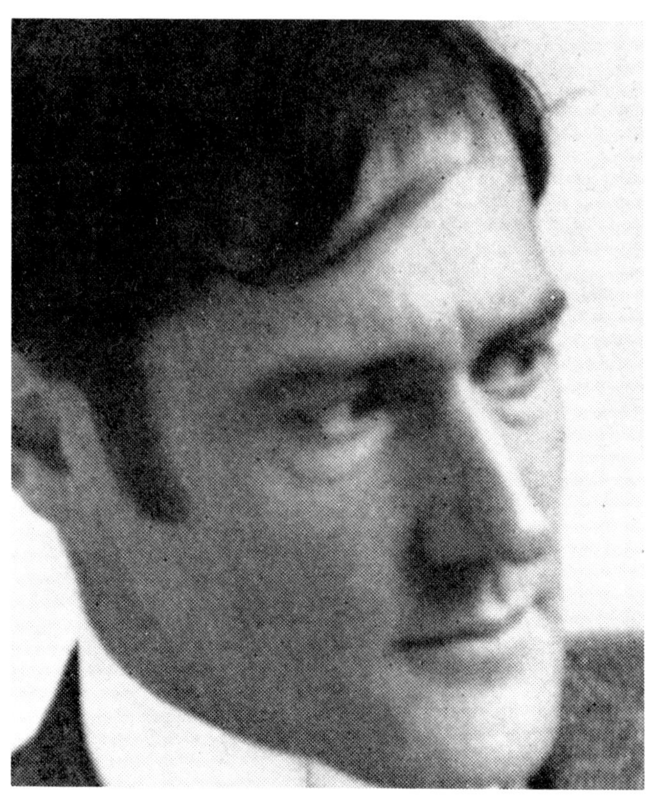

# Lyonel Feininger

1871  NEW  YORK  1956

10 **Stadt mit Sonne**
*(City with Sun)*
Watercolor, 1921
8 x 11¼″ (20.3 x 28.6 cm)
Signed lower left, titled lower center
dated lower right

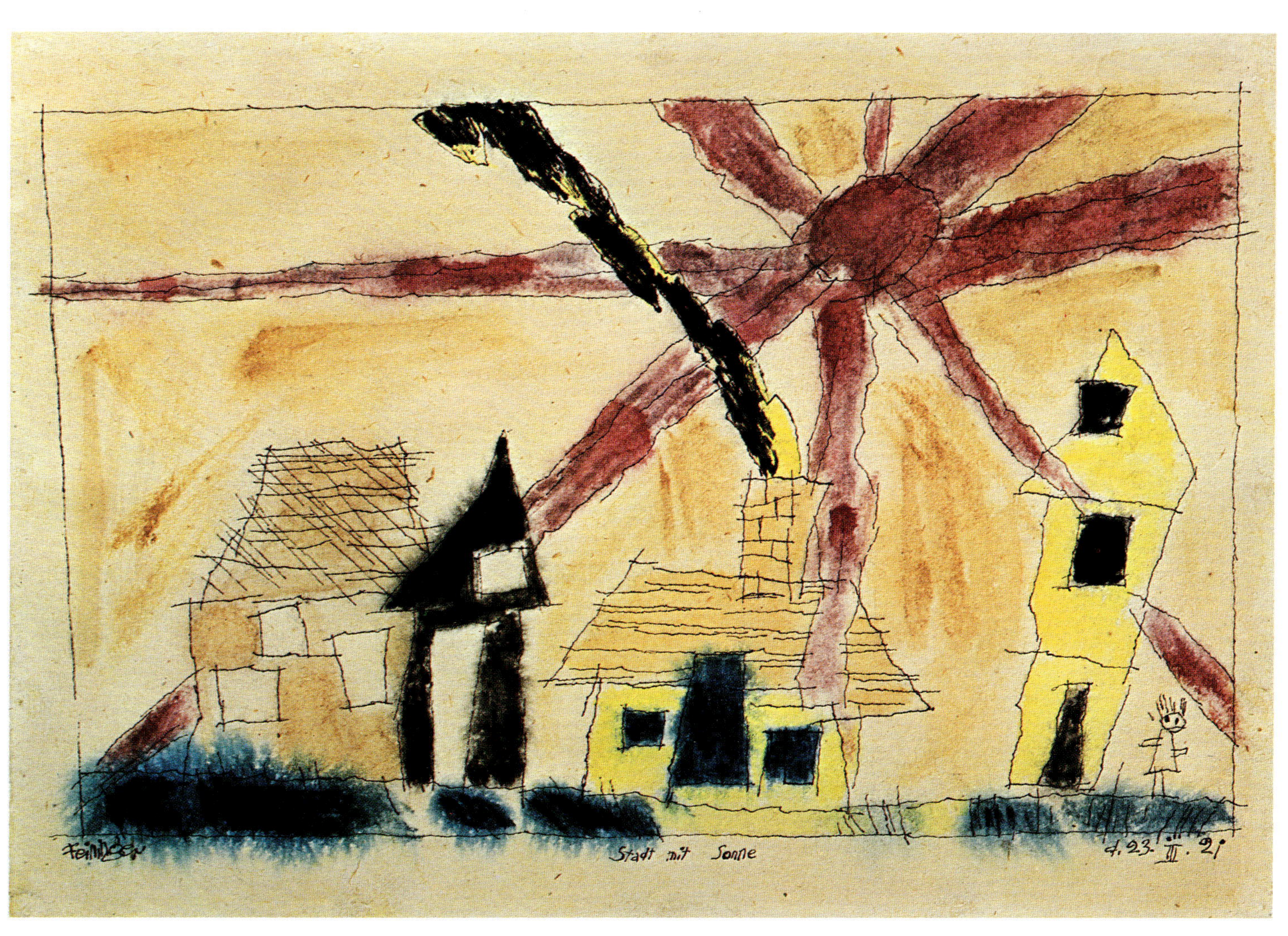
Stadt mit Sonne

# Lyonel Feininger

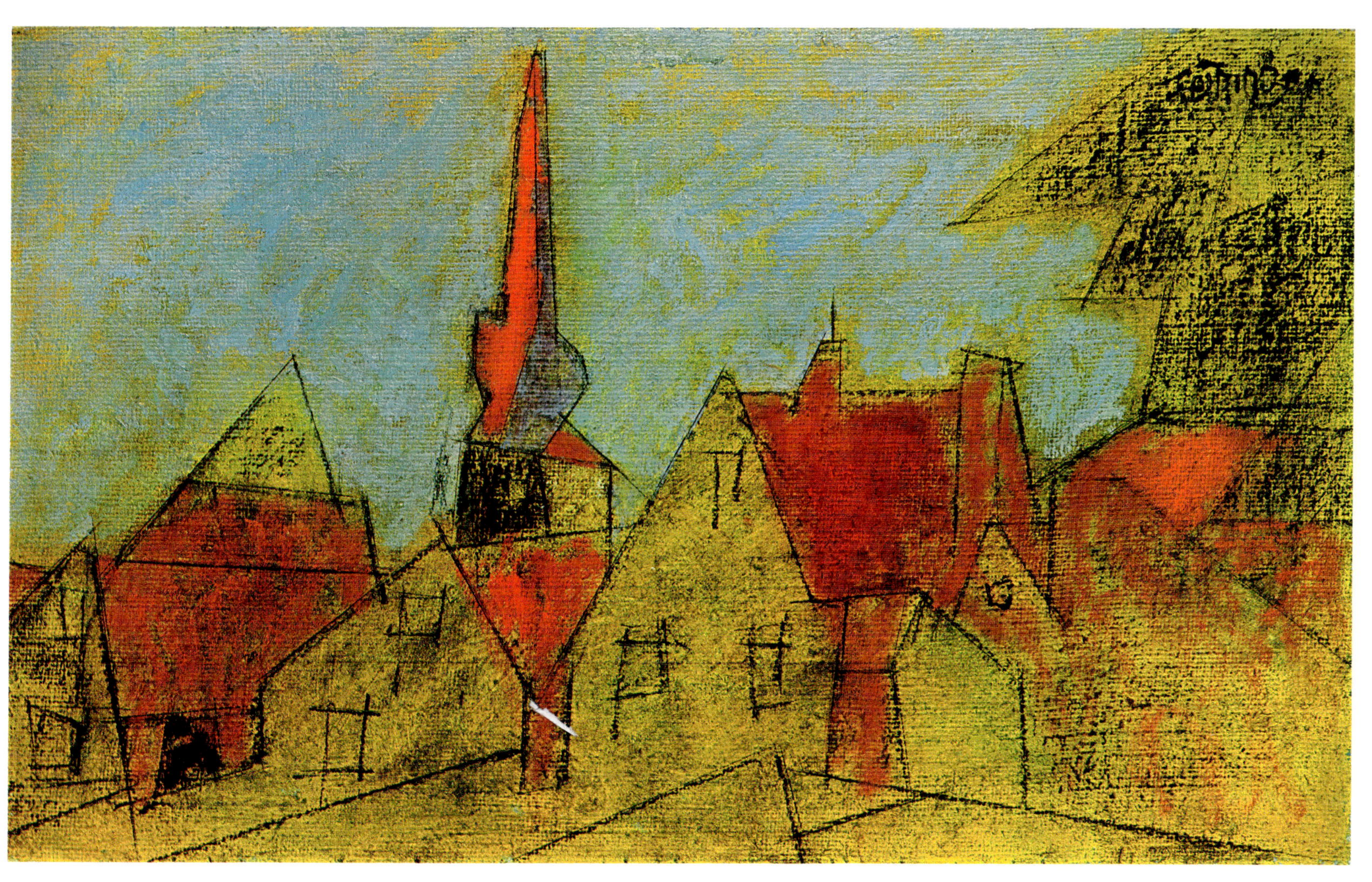

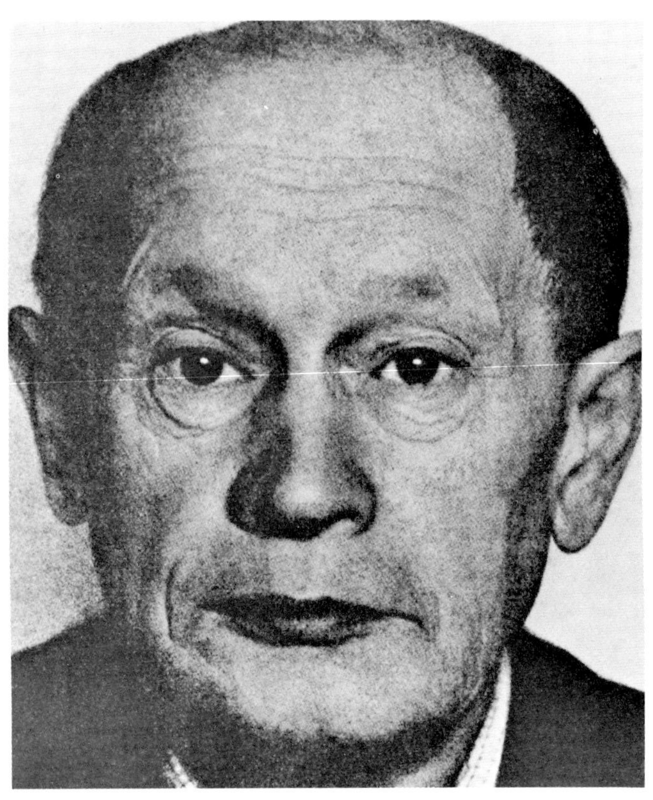

# Erich Heckel

DOEBELN 1883 - 1970 RADOLFZELL NEAR HEMMENHOFEN

14 Landschaft bei Hohenau
*(Landscape near Hohenau)*
Watercolor, 1913
15⅜ x 20⅛″ (39 x 51 cm)
Signed and dated lower right
Titled lower left

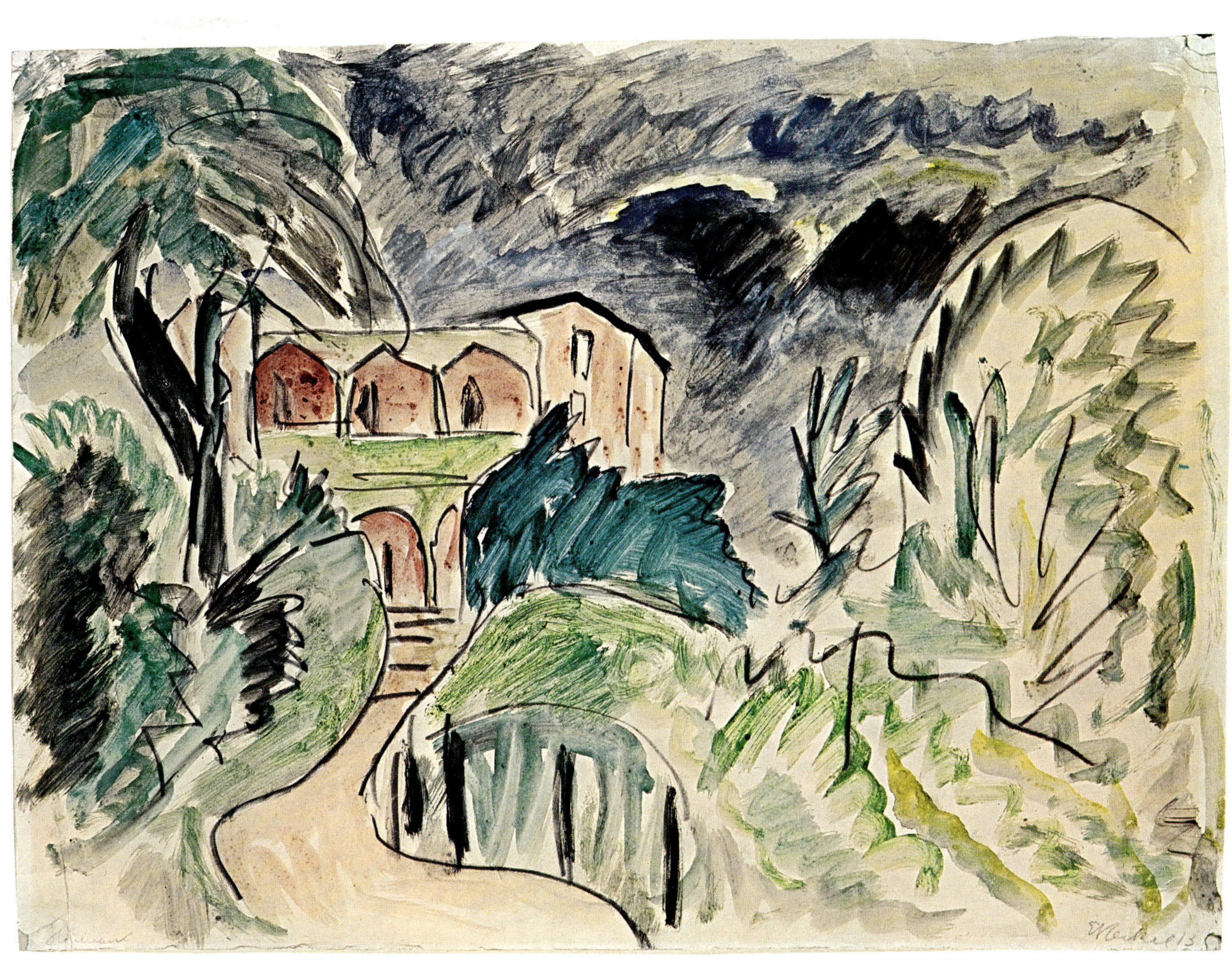

Erich Heckel



**Die Schleuse**
*(The Sluice)*
Oil on Canvas, 1913
27½ x 31½″ (70 x 80 cm)
Signed, dated and titled
on stretcher reverse

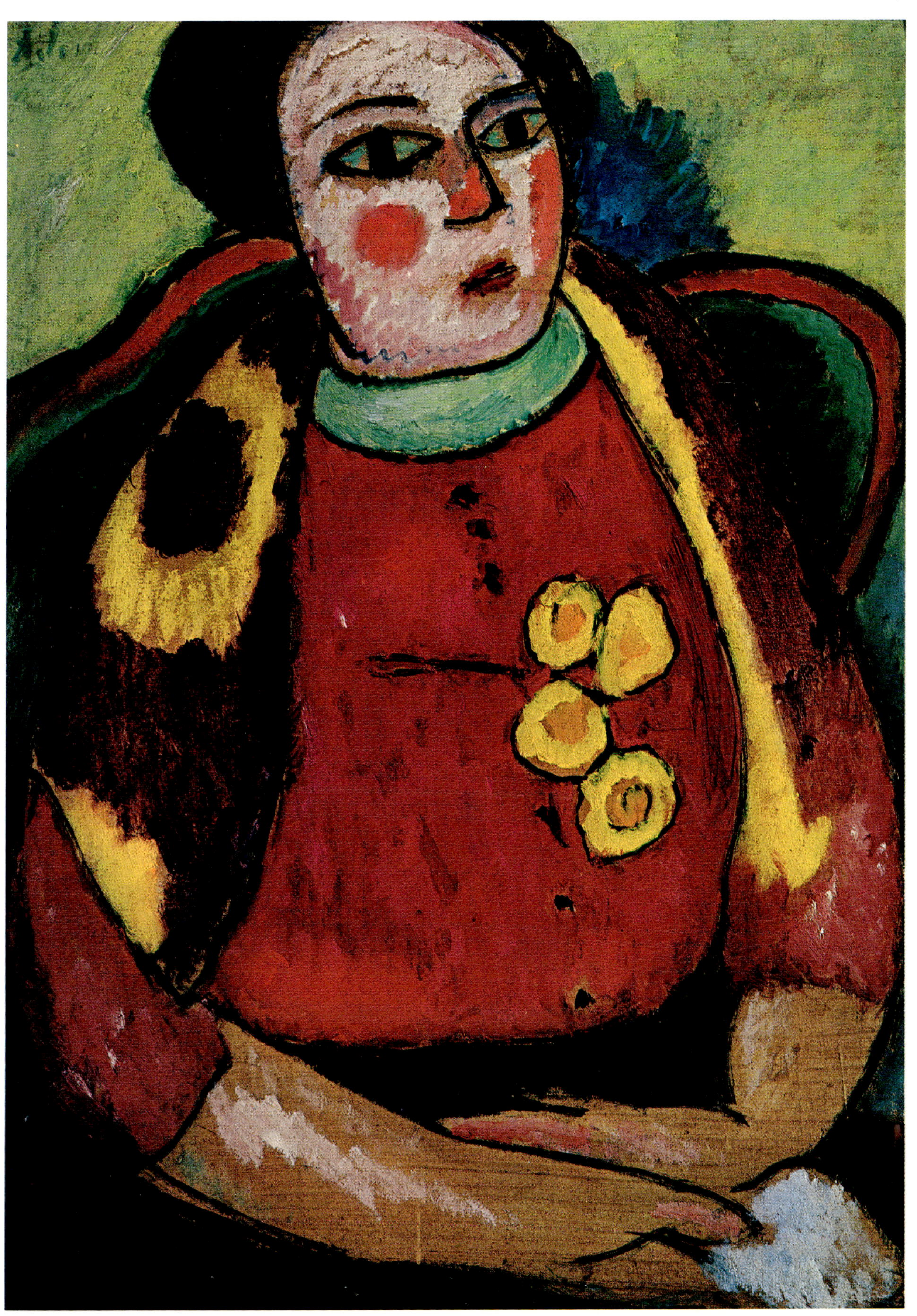

Alexej Jawlensky

21 **Konstruktiver Kopf**
*(Constructivist Head)*
Oil on board, 1932
12 x 9½″ (30.5 x 24.1 cm)
Initialed lower left, dated lower right

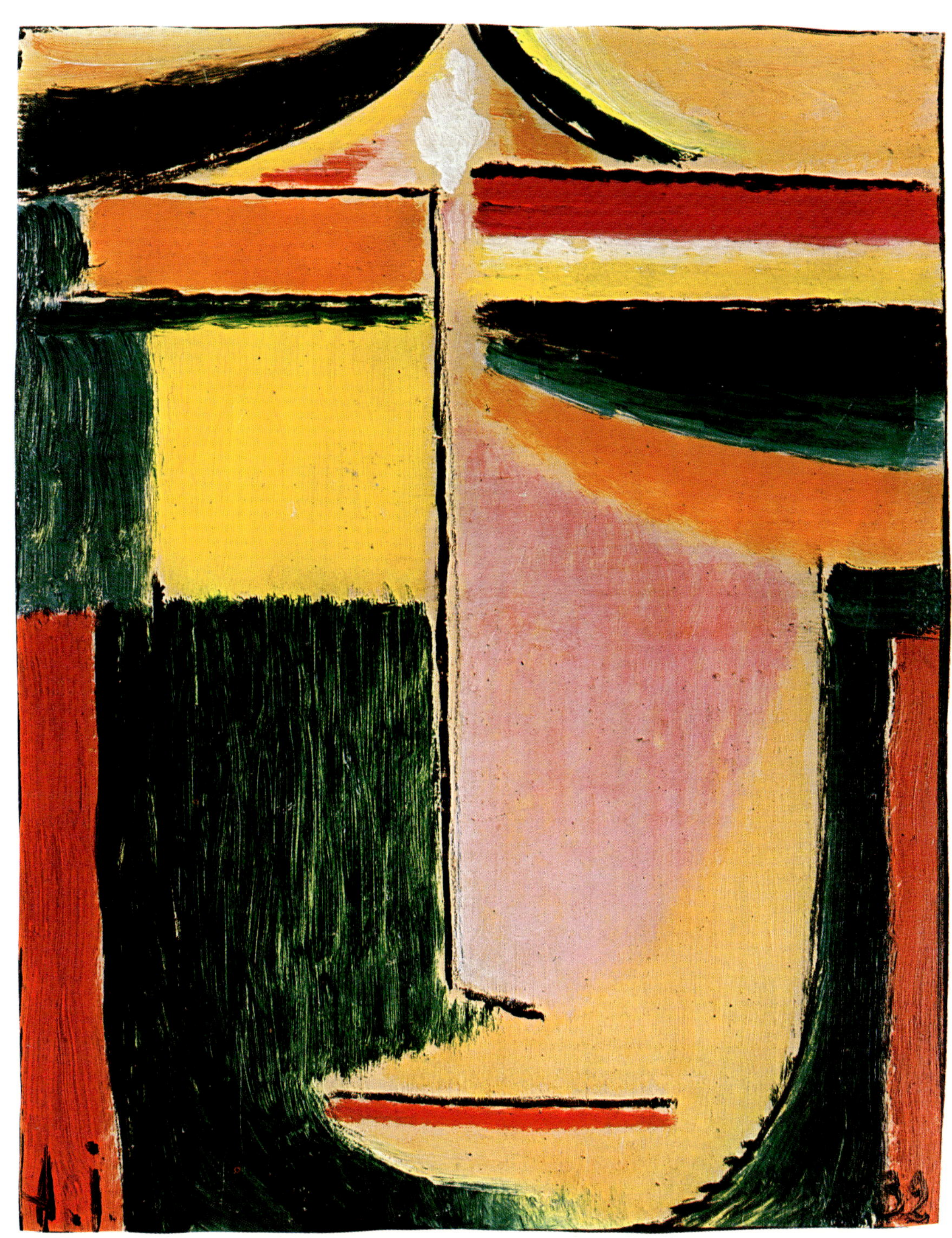

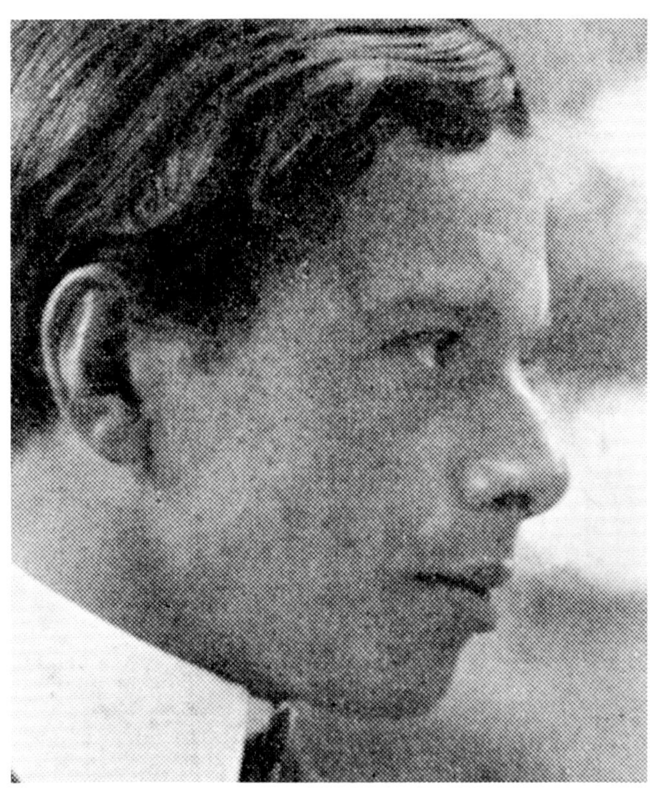

# Ernst Ludwig Kirchner

ASCHAFFENBURG 1880 - 1938 DAVOS

22 Nude Couple
Charcoal and colored crayon, 1904
16¾ x 13½″ (42.5 x 34.3 cm)
Signed and dated lower right
Estate stamp on reverse

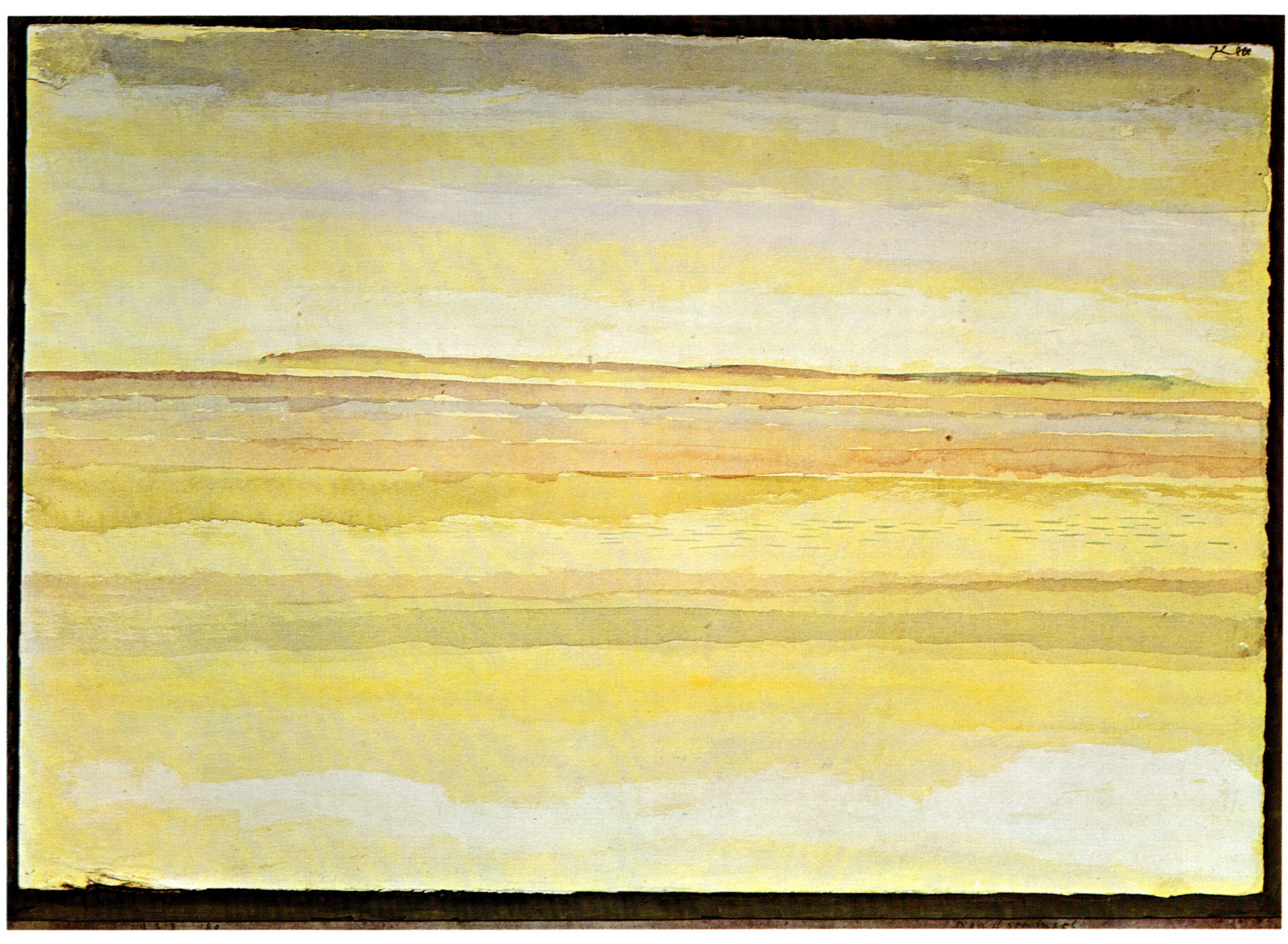

# Paul Klee

29 **Reiher**
*(Heron)*
Colored ink, 1924
11⅛ x 6″ (28.2 x 15.2 cm)
Signed lower left
Dated, numbered and titled on mount

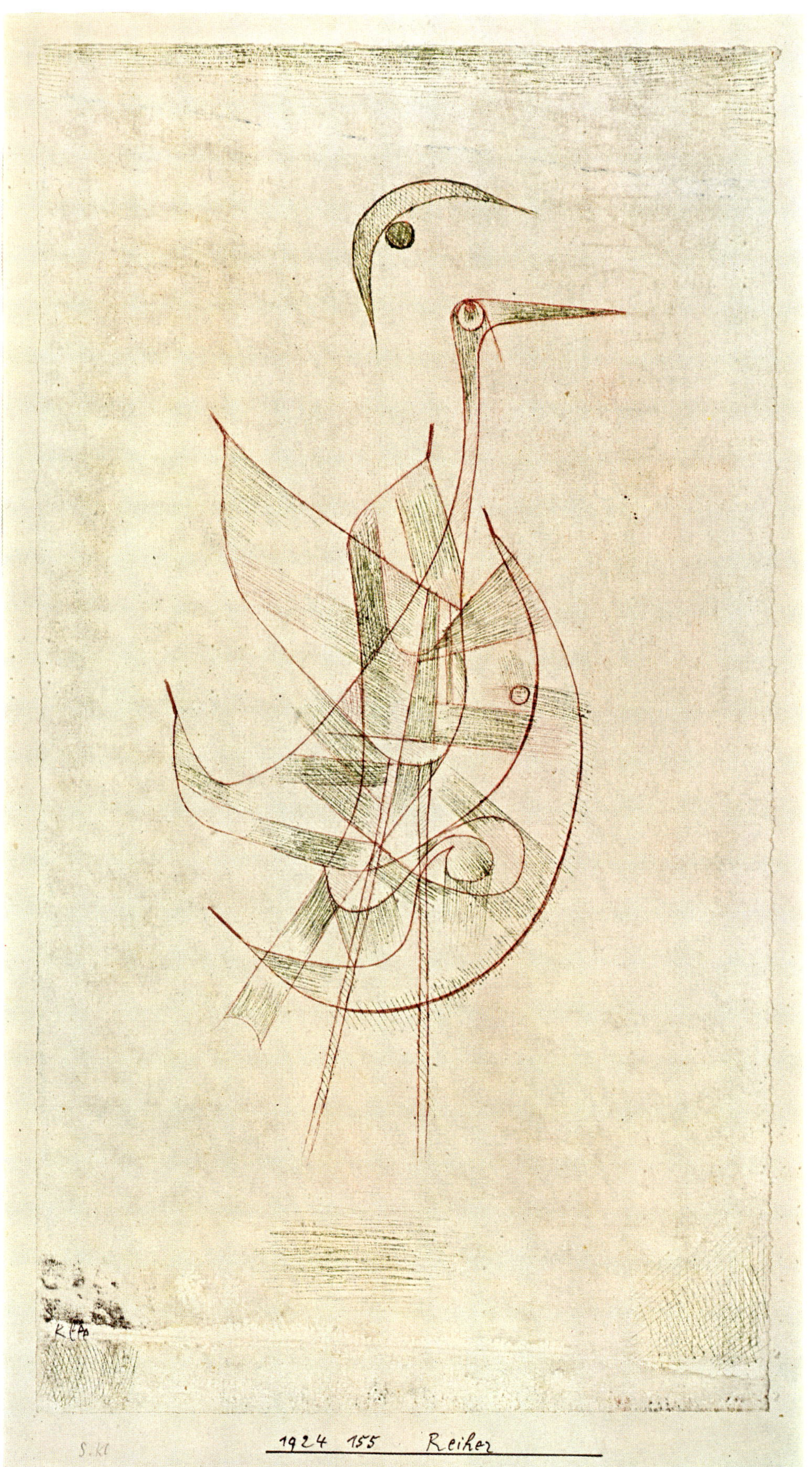

S.Kl · 1924 155 Reiher

Paul Klee

30 Gladiolen Stilleben
*(Gladiolas - Stillife)*
Watercolor, 1932
24½ x 18¾″ (62.2 x 47.6 cm)
Signed upper right
Dated, numbered and titled on mount

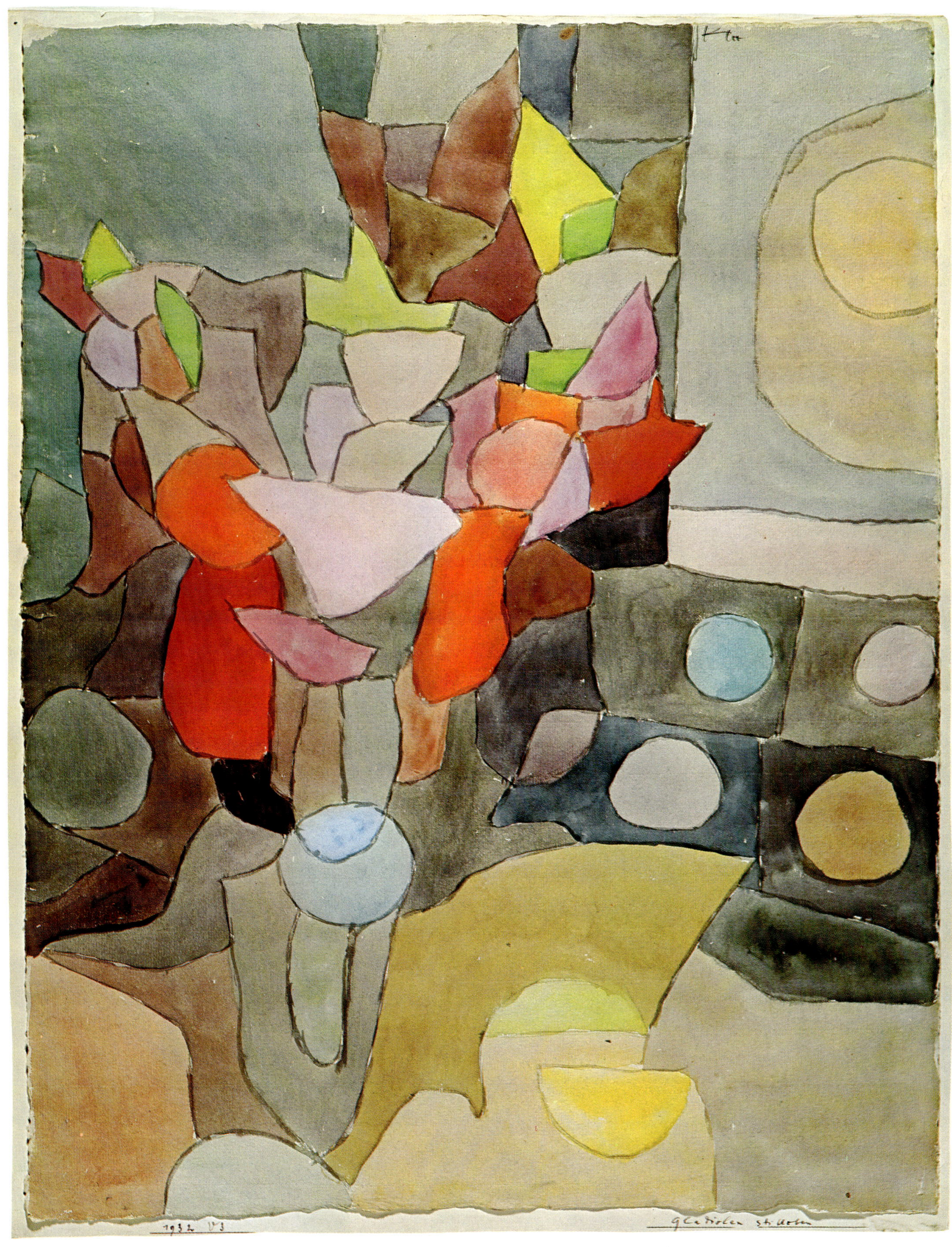

Klee
1932 N3
Gladiolen stilleben

# Paul Klee

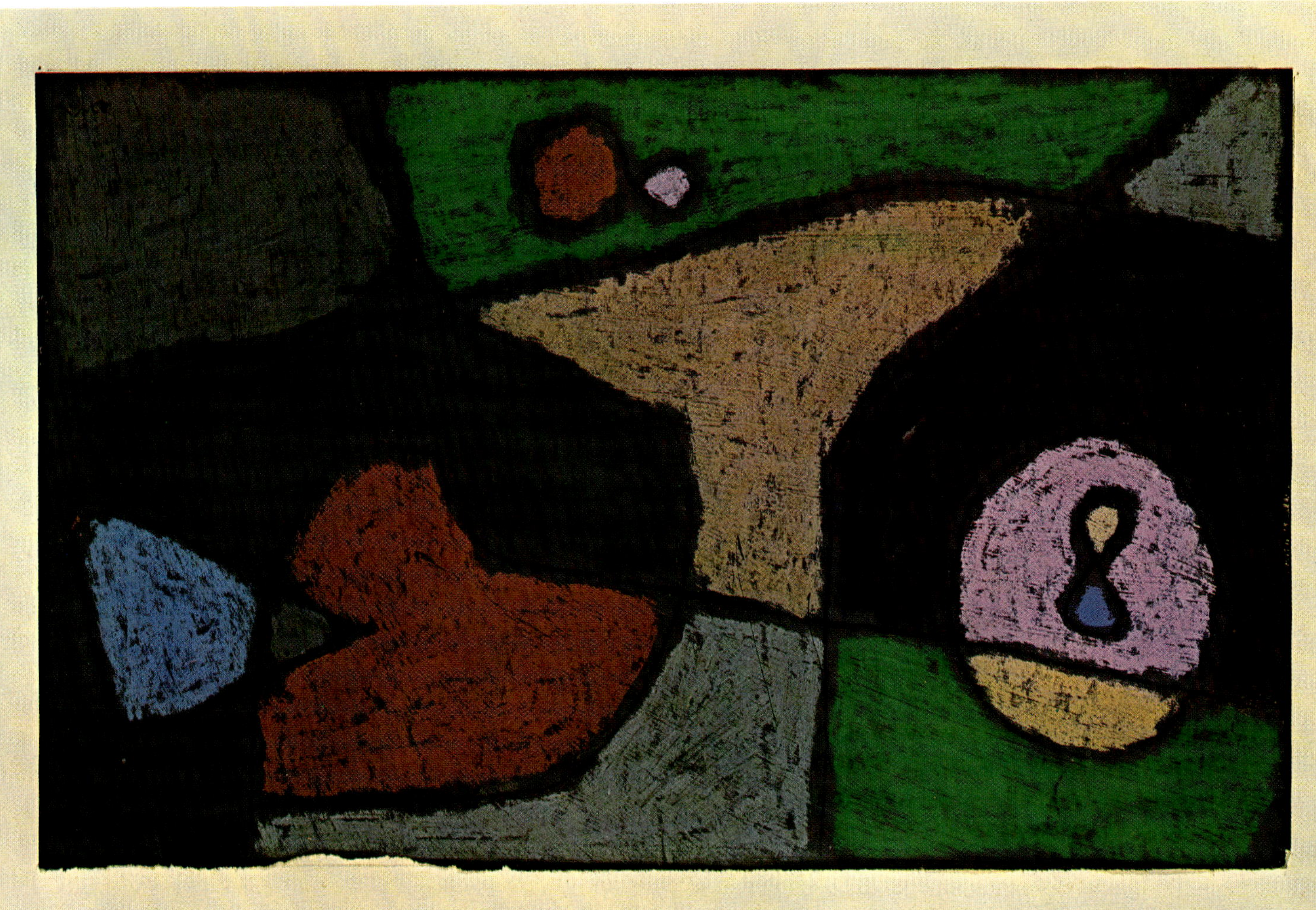

1933 48    vom Baum

# Paul Klee

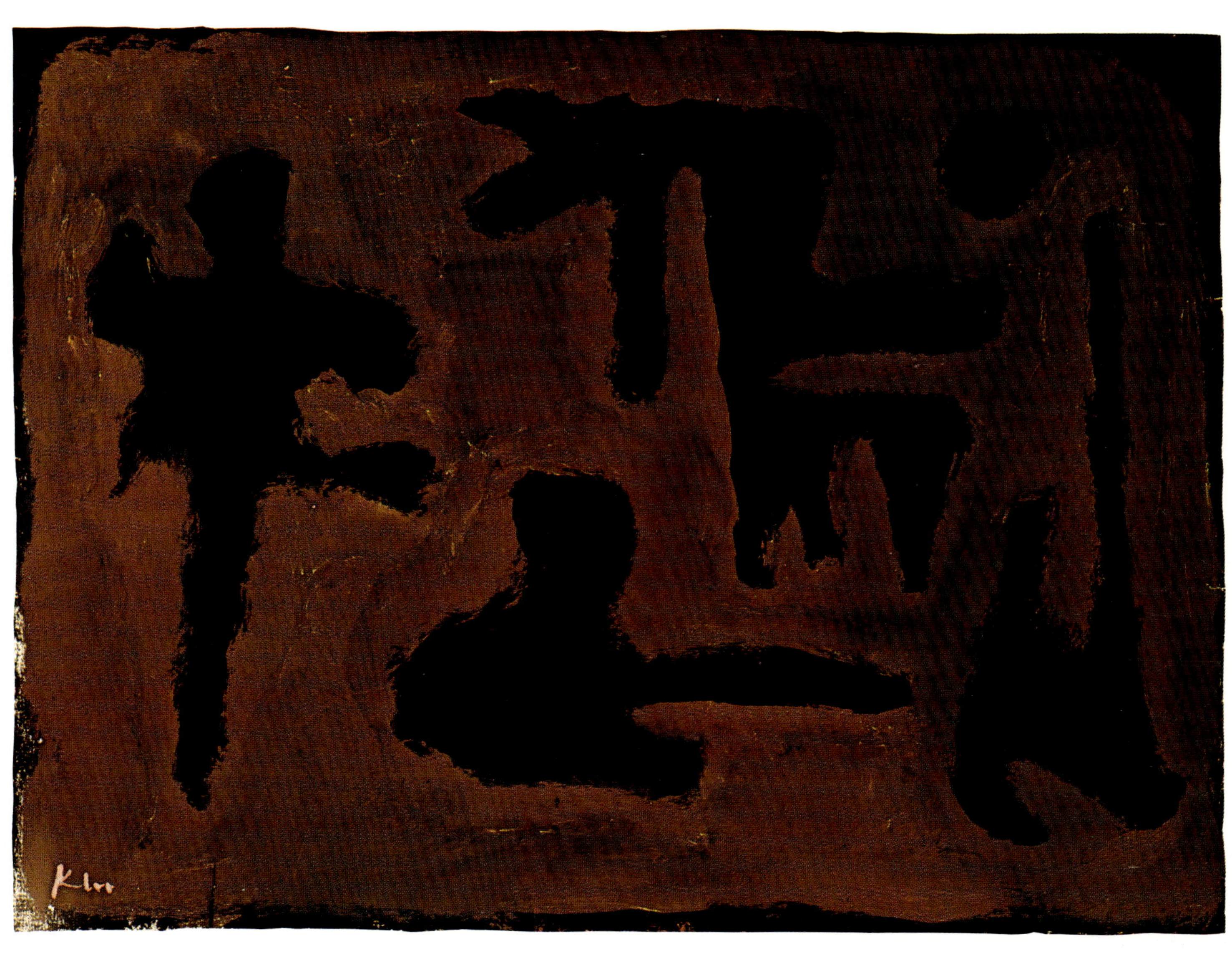

# Paul Klee

33 Landschaft zwischen Winter und Frühling
*(Landscape Between Winter and Spring)*
Mixed media on paper mounted on canvas, 1935
24¾ x 18⅞″ (62.9 x 48 cm)
Signed upper right

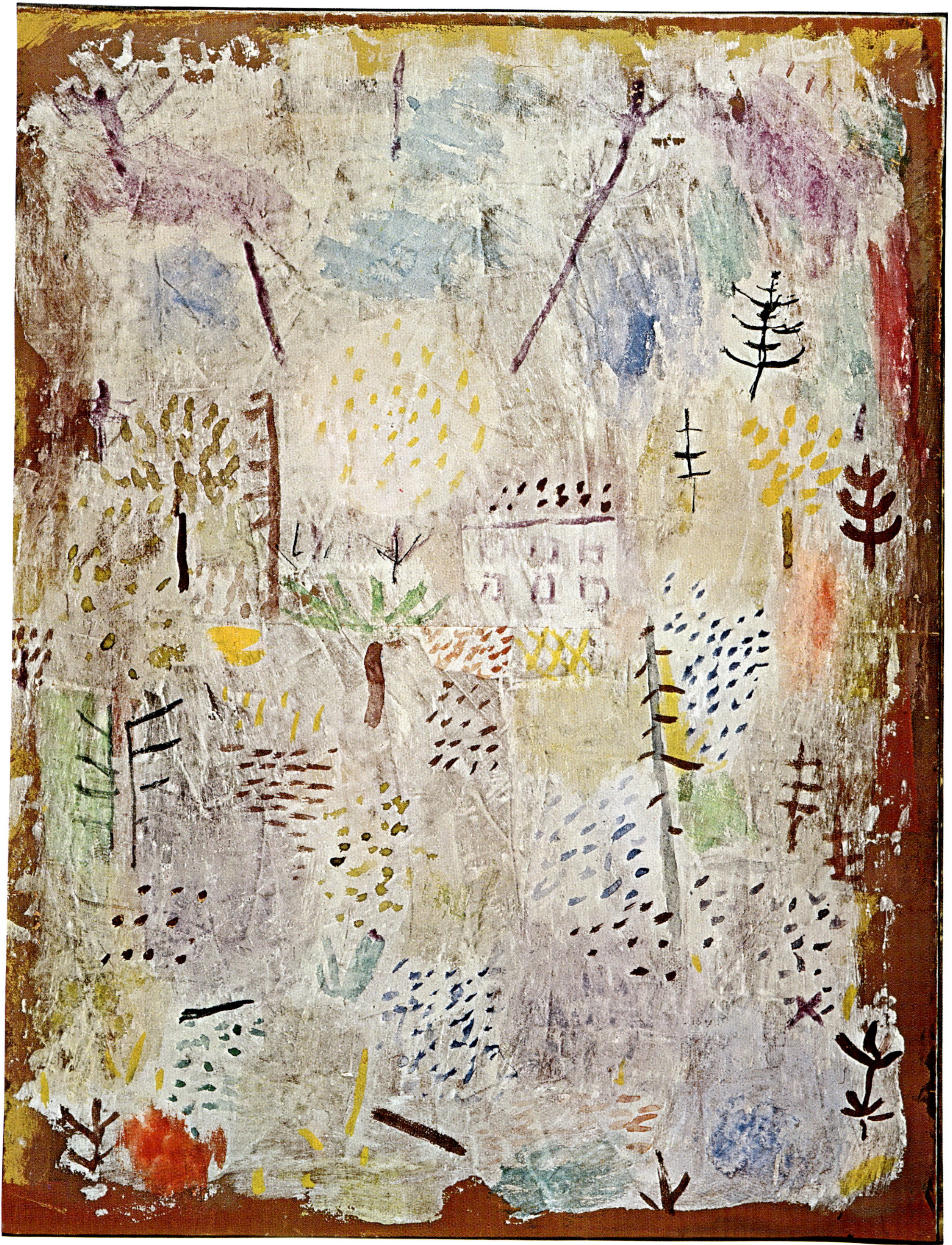

Paul Klee

34 **Drei Masken**
*(Three Masks)*
Pastel on cloth, 1936
12½ x 22¾″ (31.7 x 57.8 cm)
Signed lower right
Dated, numbered and titled on mount

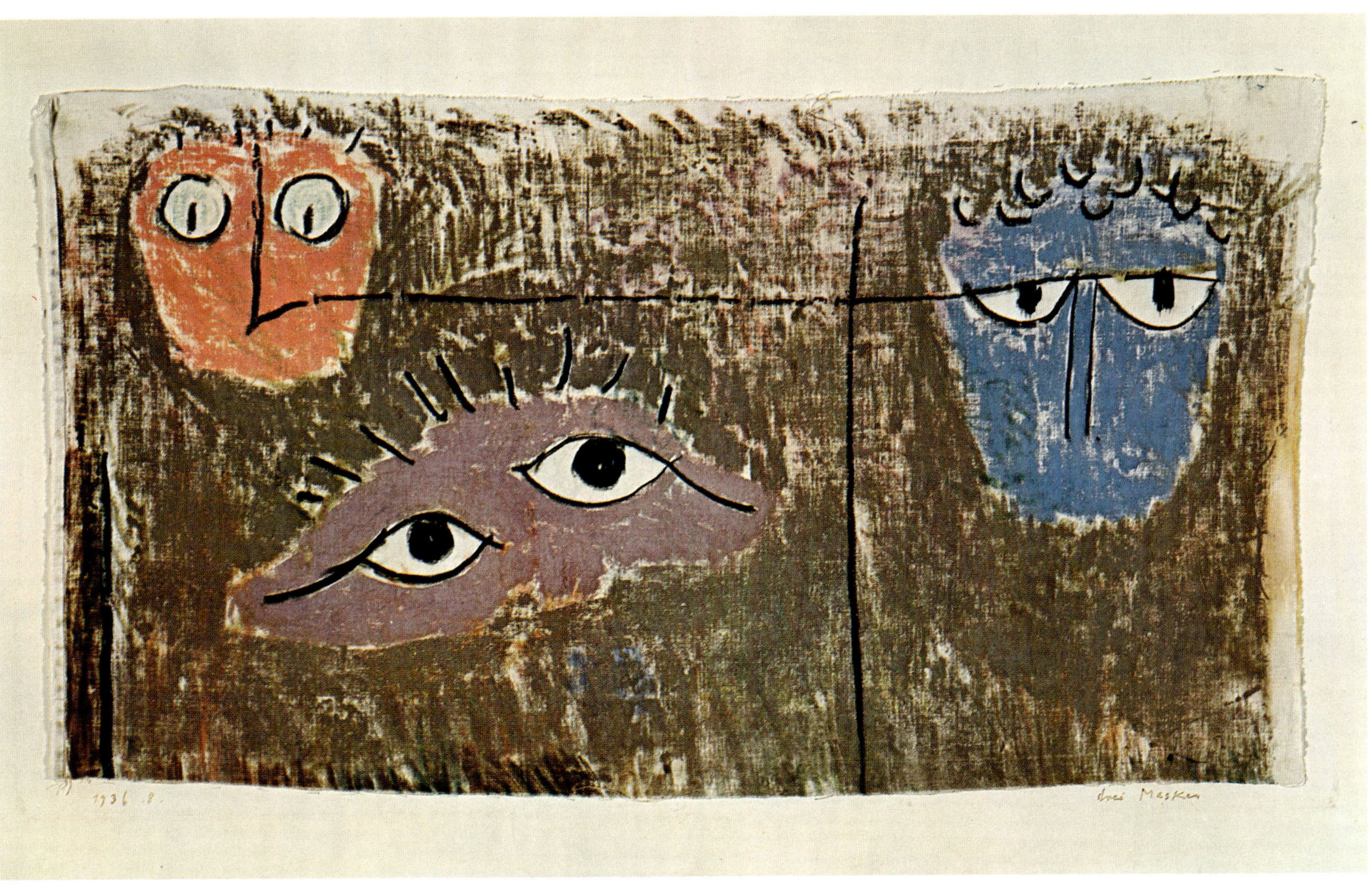

# Paul Klee

35  Stolz
    *(Pride)*
    Ink wash, 1937
    15¾ x 9⅜″ (40 x 23.8 cm)
    Signed upper right
    Dated, numbered and titled on mount

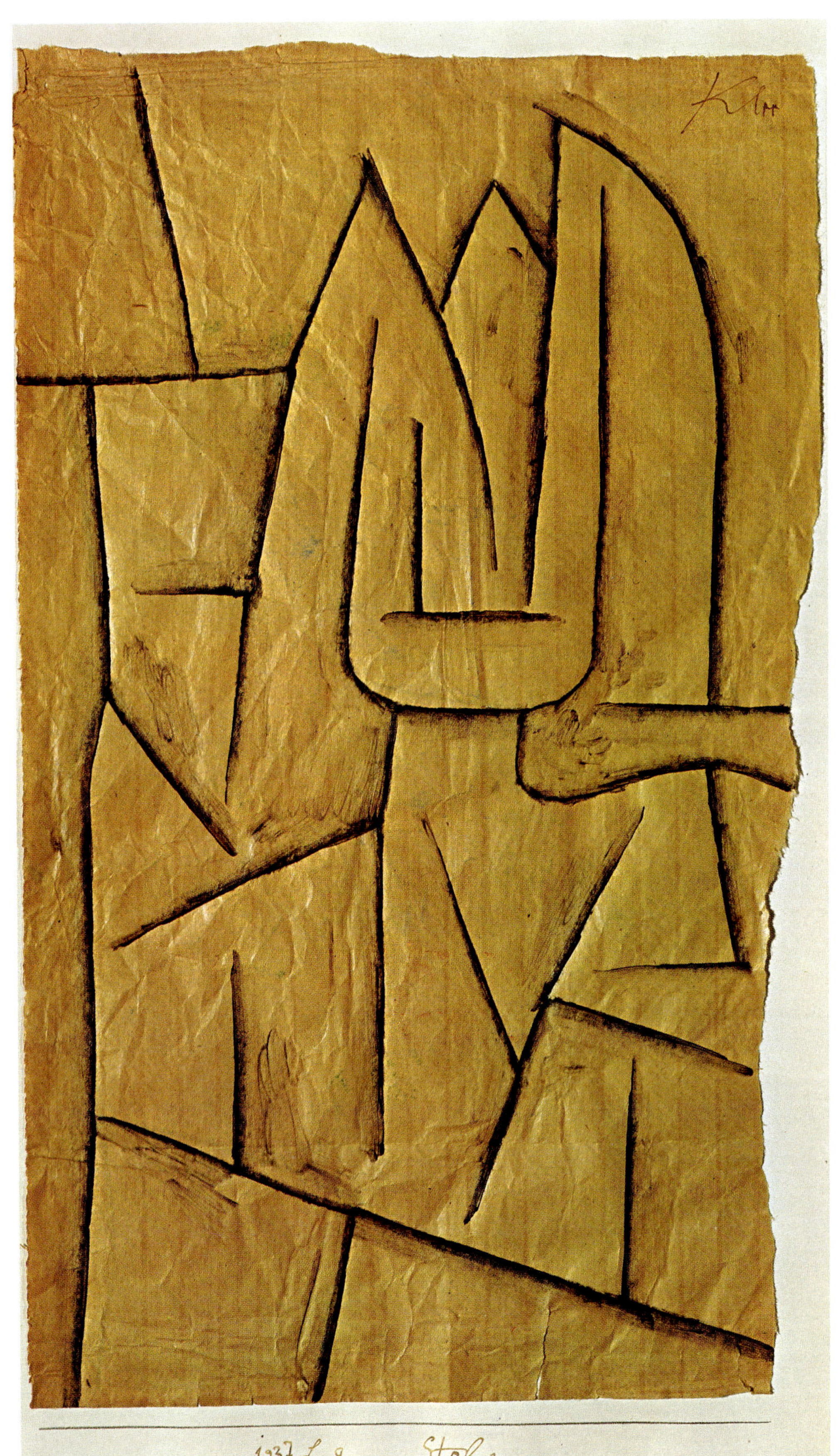

1937. L 9.    Stolz

Paul Klee

36 Ein Kind und das Groteske
*(A Child and the Grotesque)*
Colored crayon, 1938
11¾ x 8⅛" (29.8 x 20.6 cm)
Signed upper right
Dated, numbered and titled on mount

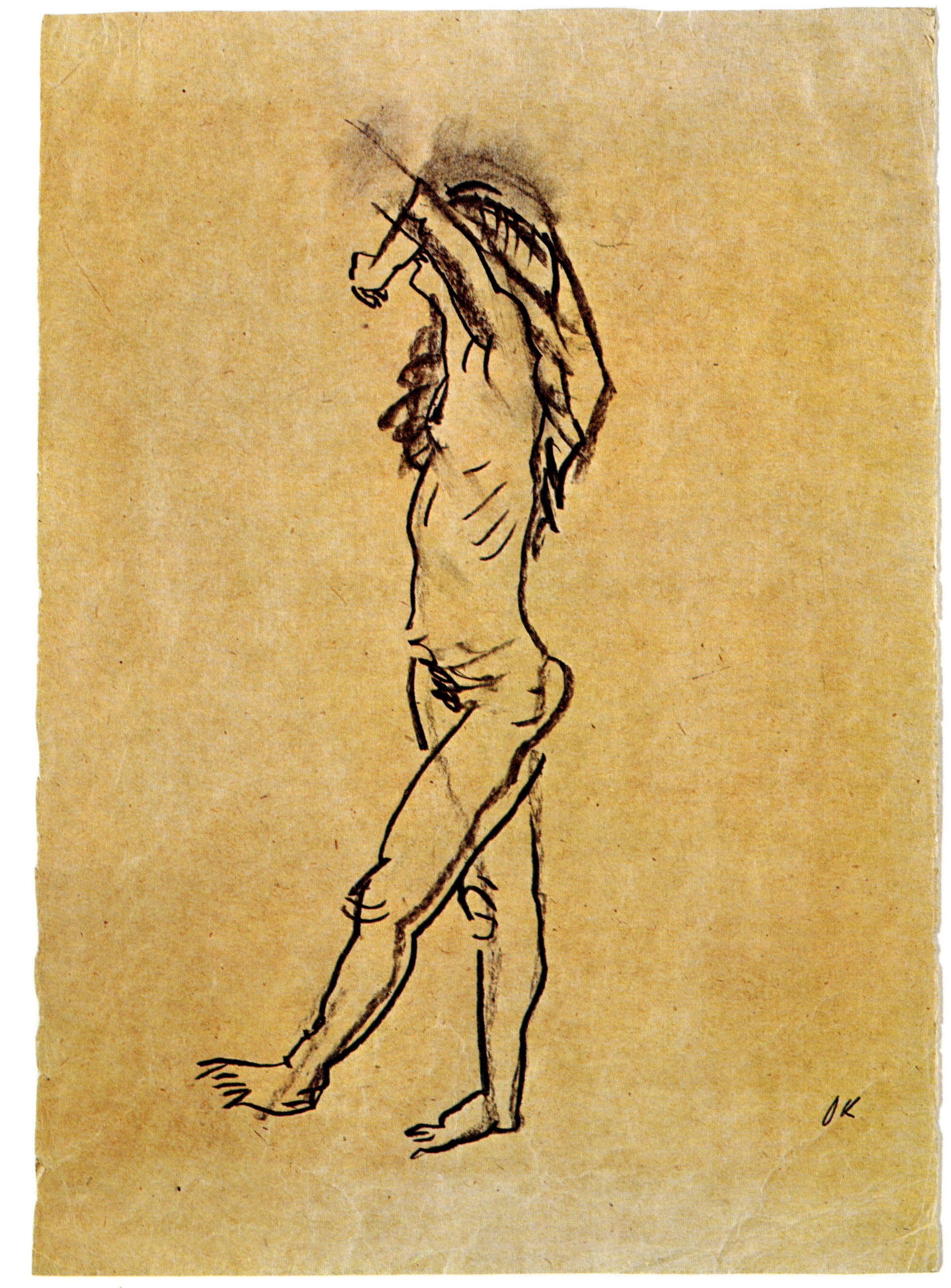

Oskar Kokoschka

40 Portrait of Frau Hirsch
Oil on canvas, 1908
35⅝ x 28⅜″ (90.5 x 72 cm)
Initialed lower right

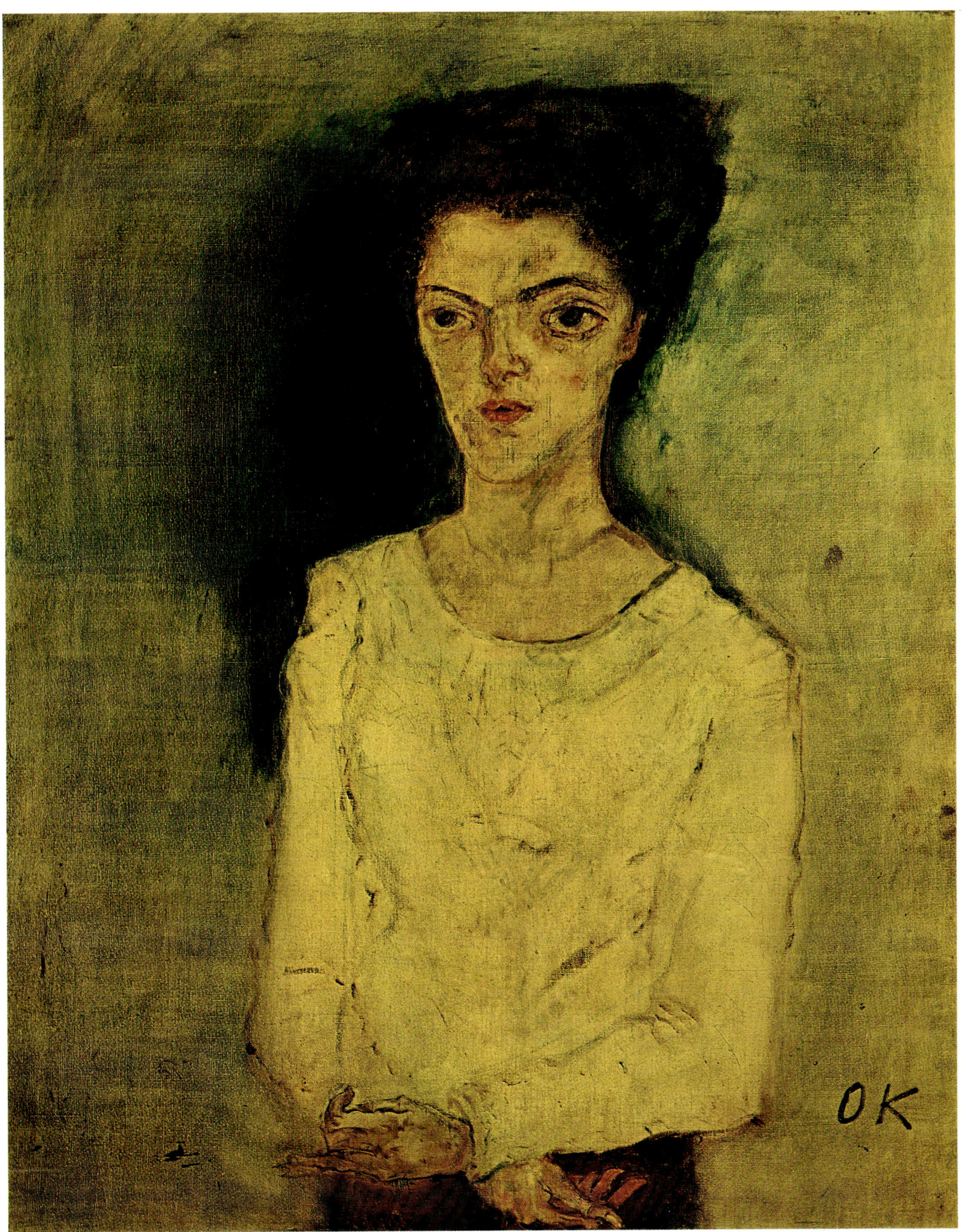

# Oskar Kokoschka



**Reclining Nude**
Charcoal, 1911
12⅜ x 17¾″ (31.4 x 45 cm)
Initialed lower left

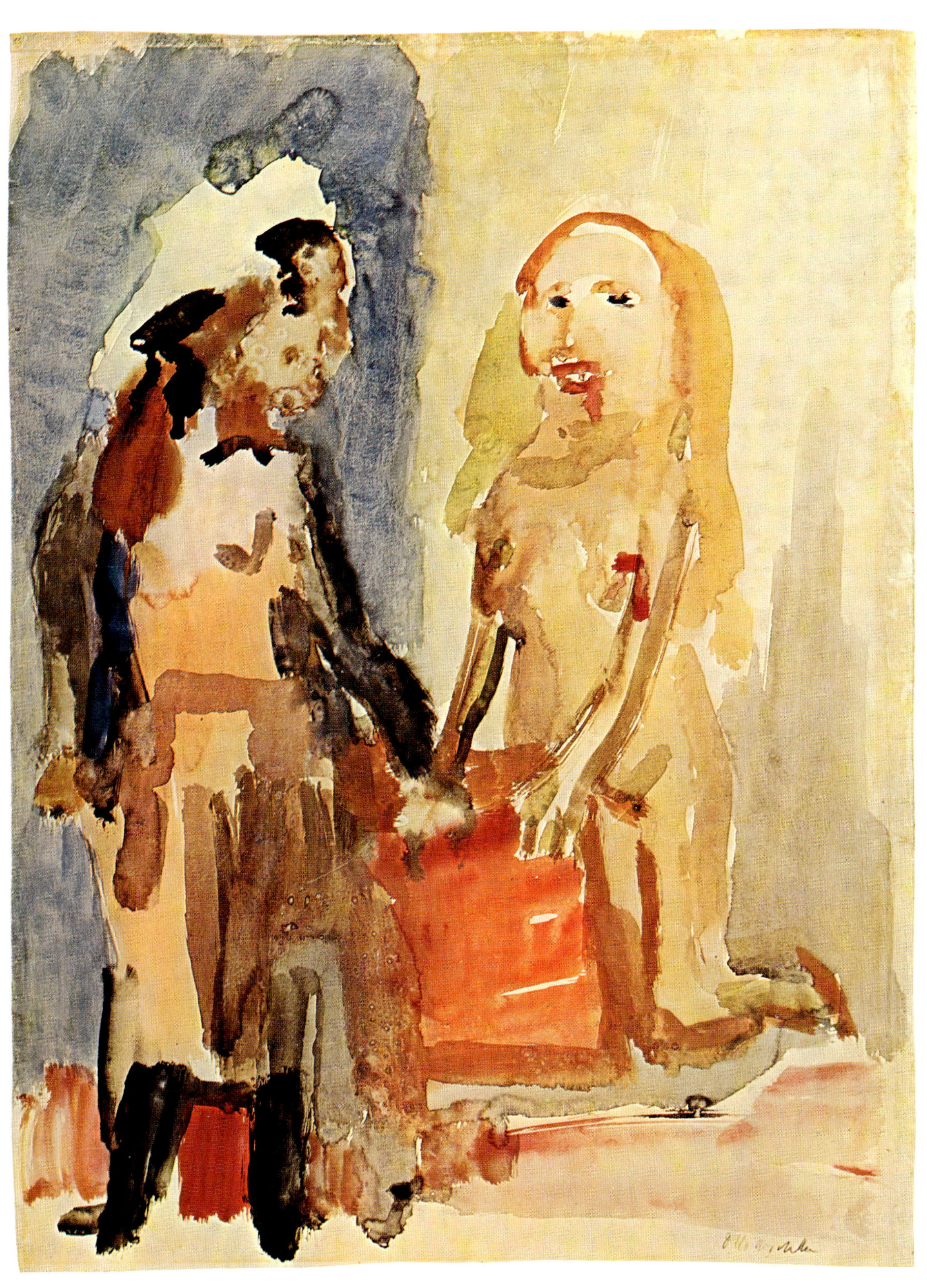

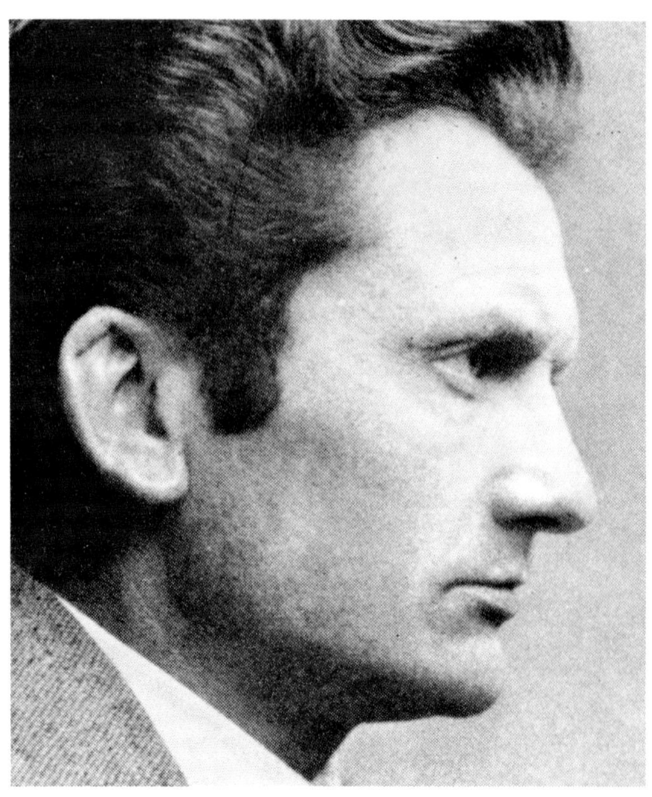

# Wilhelm Lehmbruck

DUISBURG 1881 - 1919 BERLIN

44  Head of a Thinker
Stone, 1918
25⅜ x 22½ x 11¾″
(64.5 x 57.1 x 29.8 cm)
One of three casts

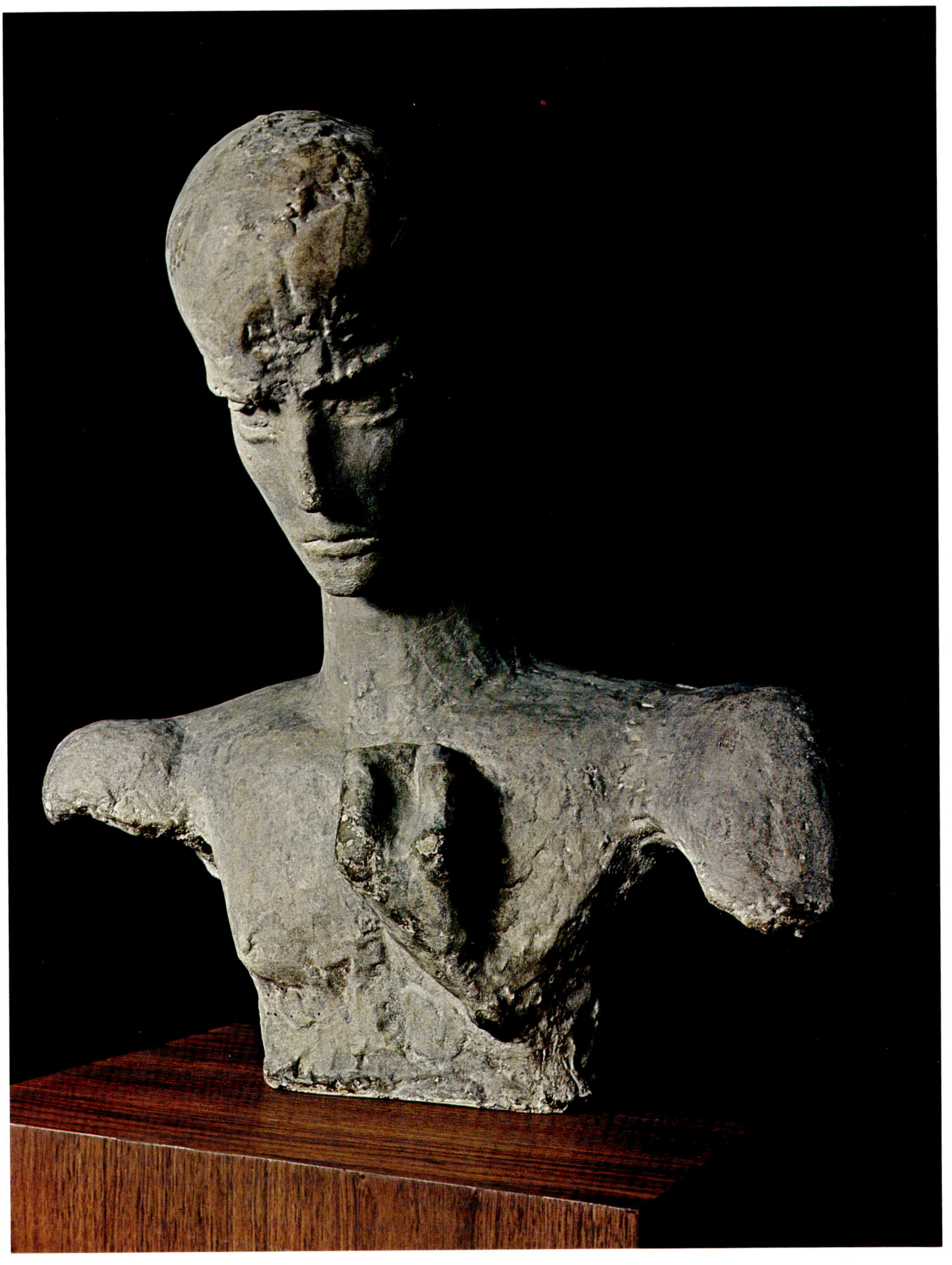

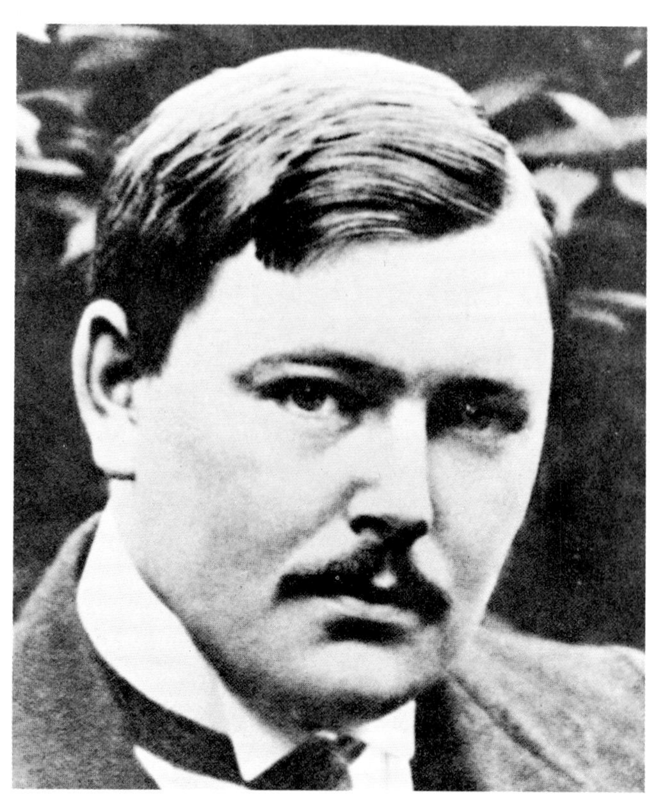

# August Macke



45   **Portrait of the Artist's Wife**
Oil on wood, 1909
21⅝ x 17¾″ (55 x 45 cm)

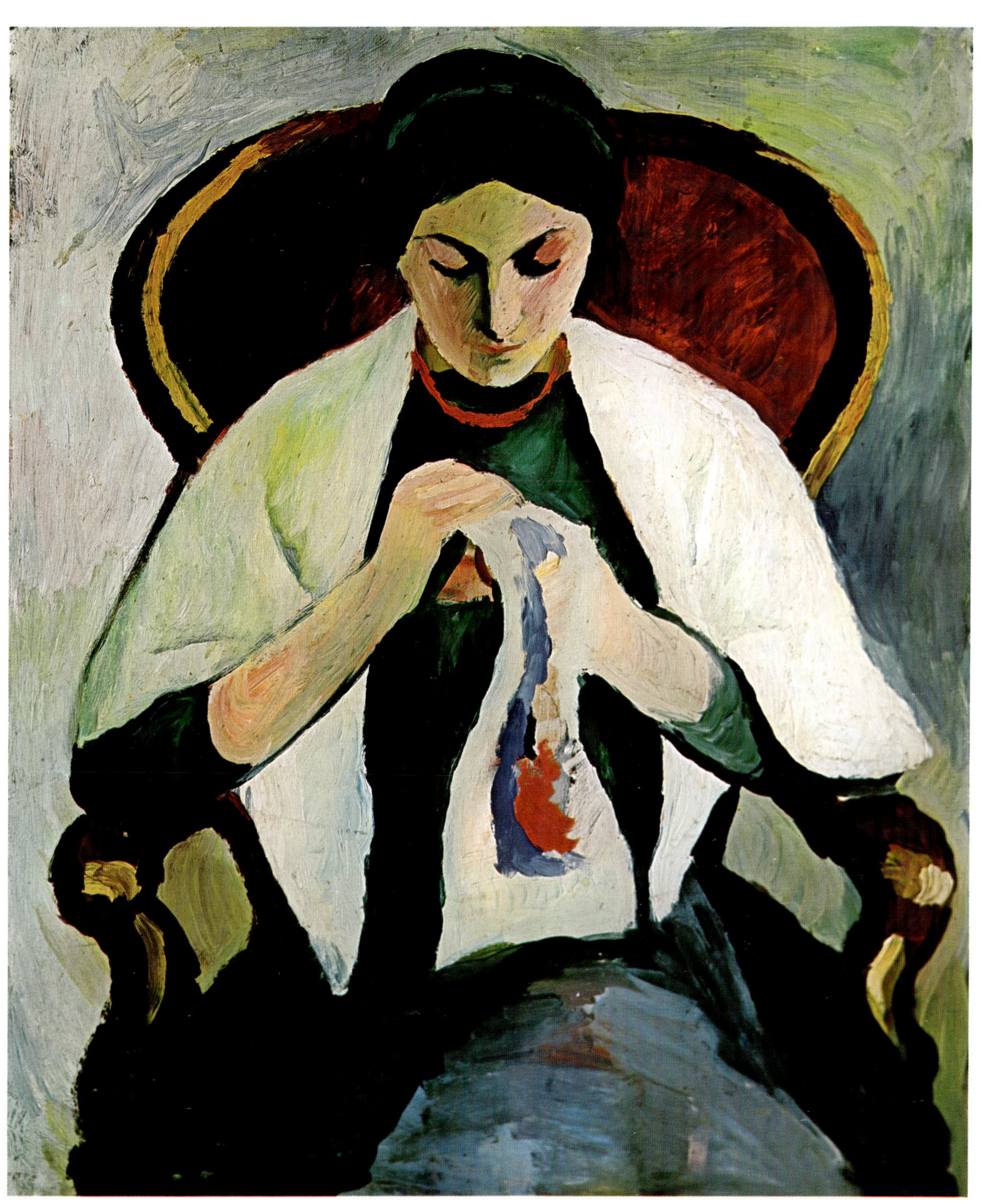

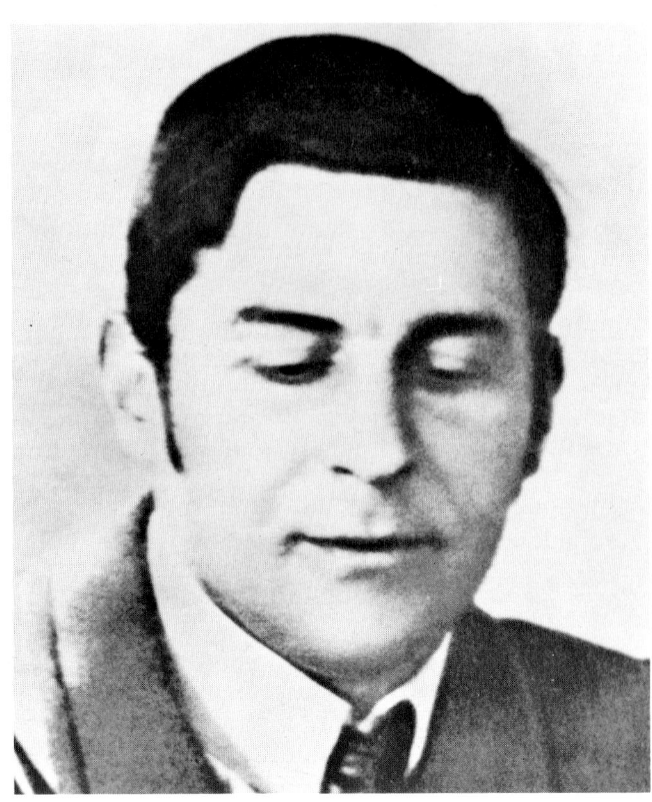

# Franz Marc

MUNICH 1880 - 1916 VERDUN

46  Rote Rehe
*(Red Deer)*
Oil on canvas, 1910
34¼ x 34⅝″ (87 x 88 cm)

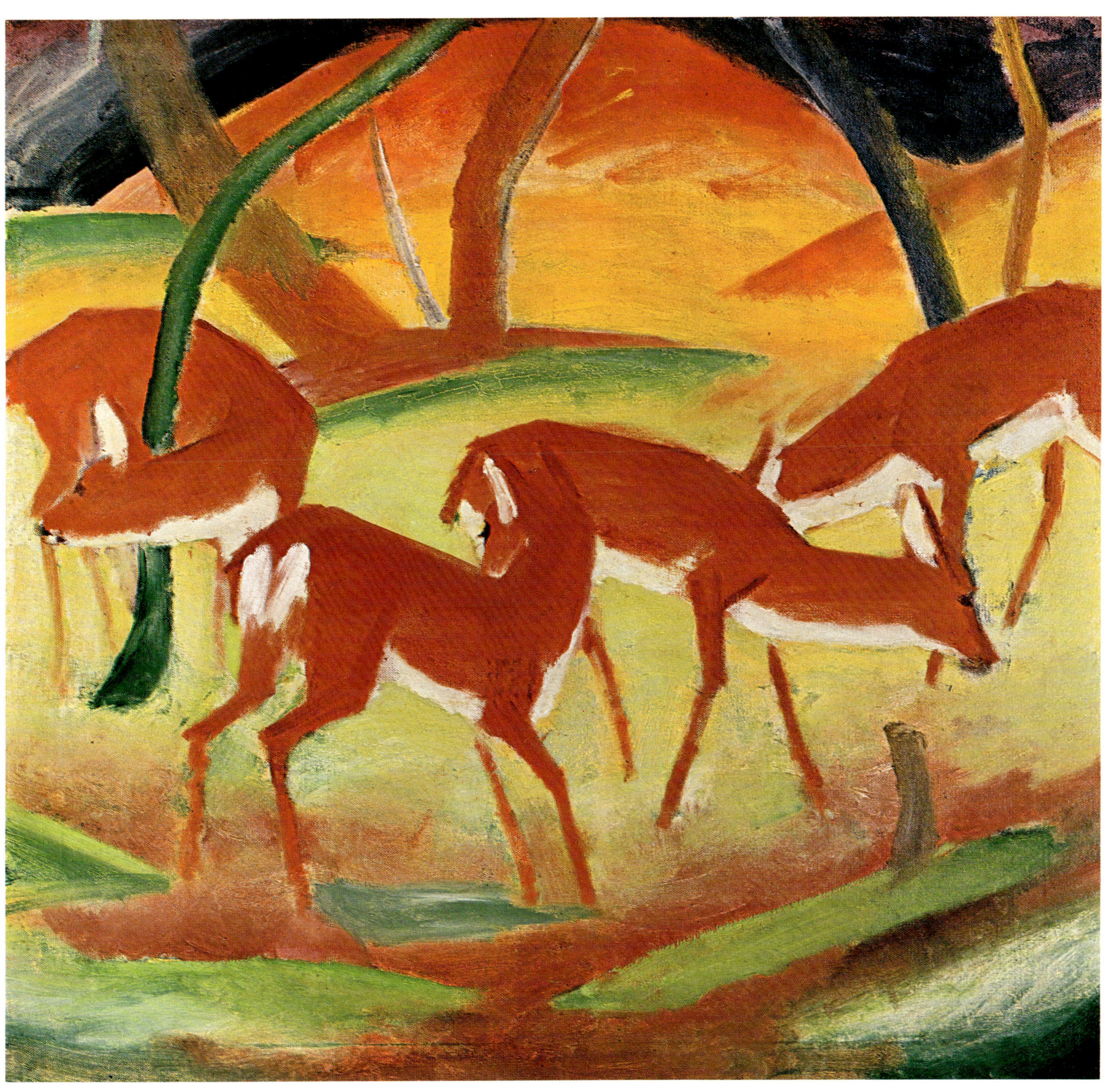

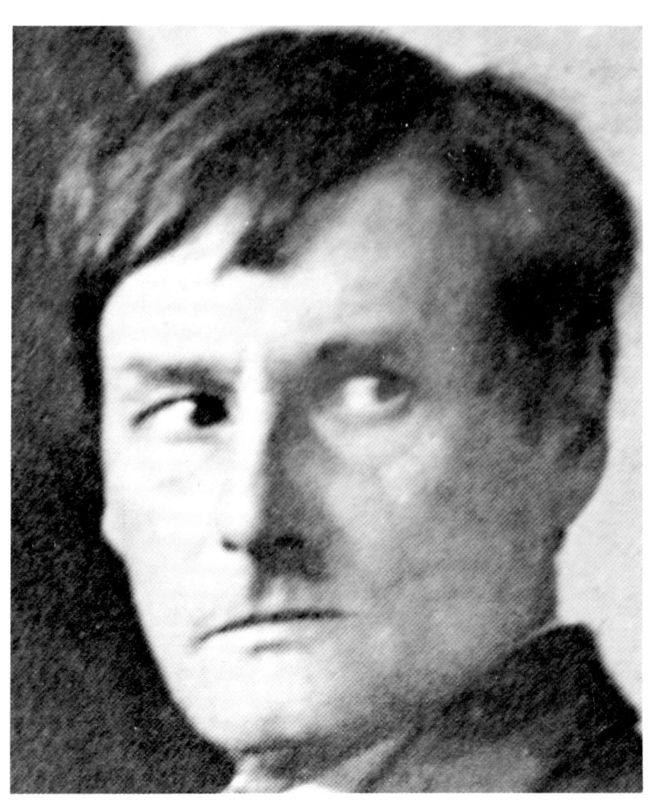

# Otto Mueller

LIEBAU 1874 - 1930 BRESLAU

**47** Two Nudes in the Forest
Watercolor and crayon on paper
26½ x 20¼″ (67.3 x 51.4 cm)
Signed lower right

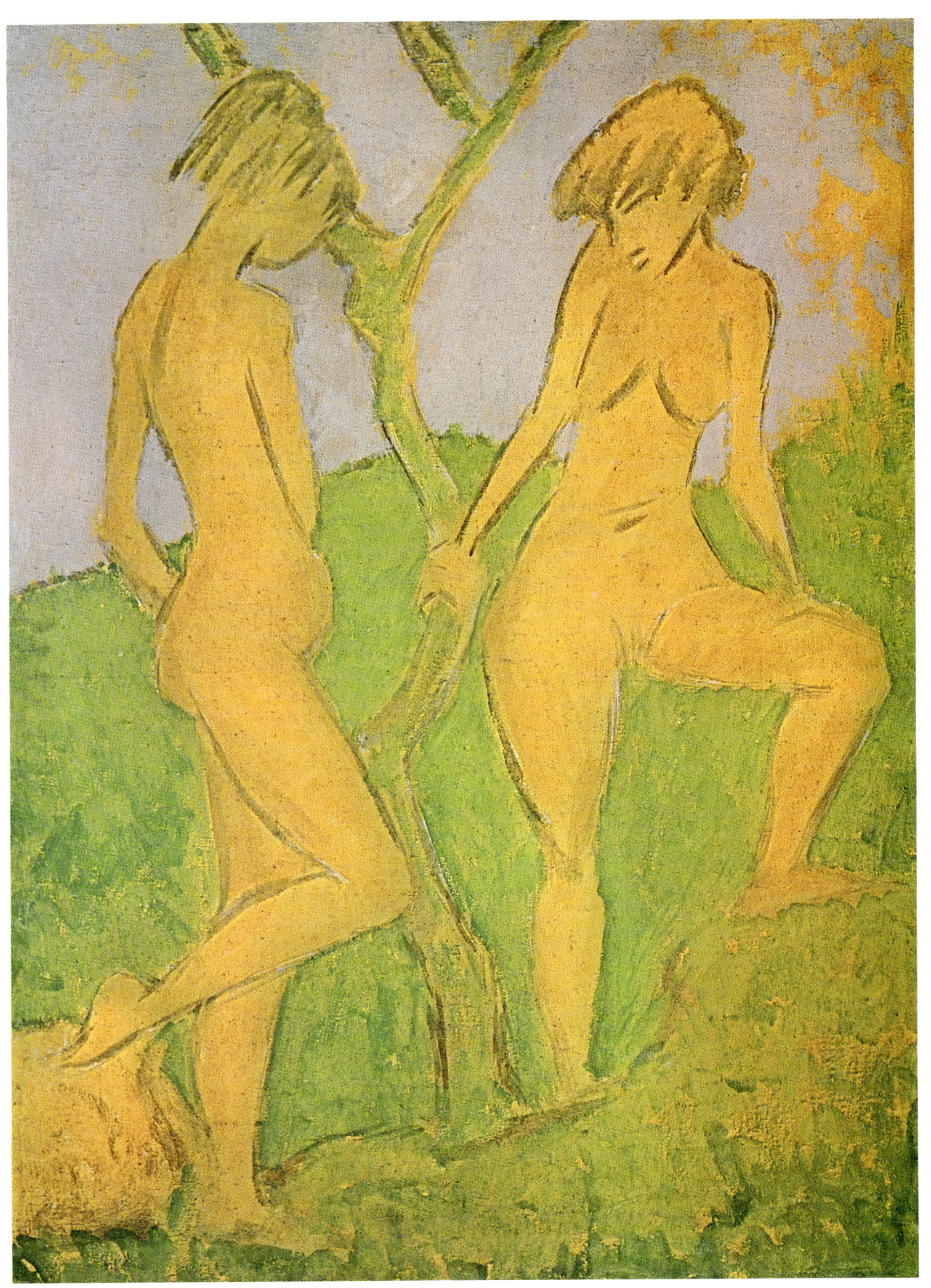

# Otto Mueller

**50** **Girl with Green Scarf**
Leimfarbe (Pigments with glue)
on canvas, 1929/30
65 x 23⅝″ (165 x 60 cm)

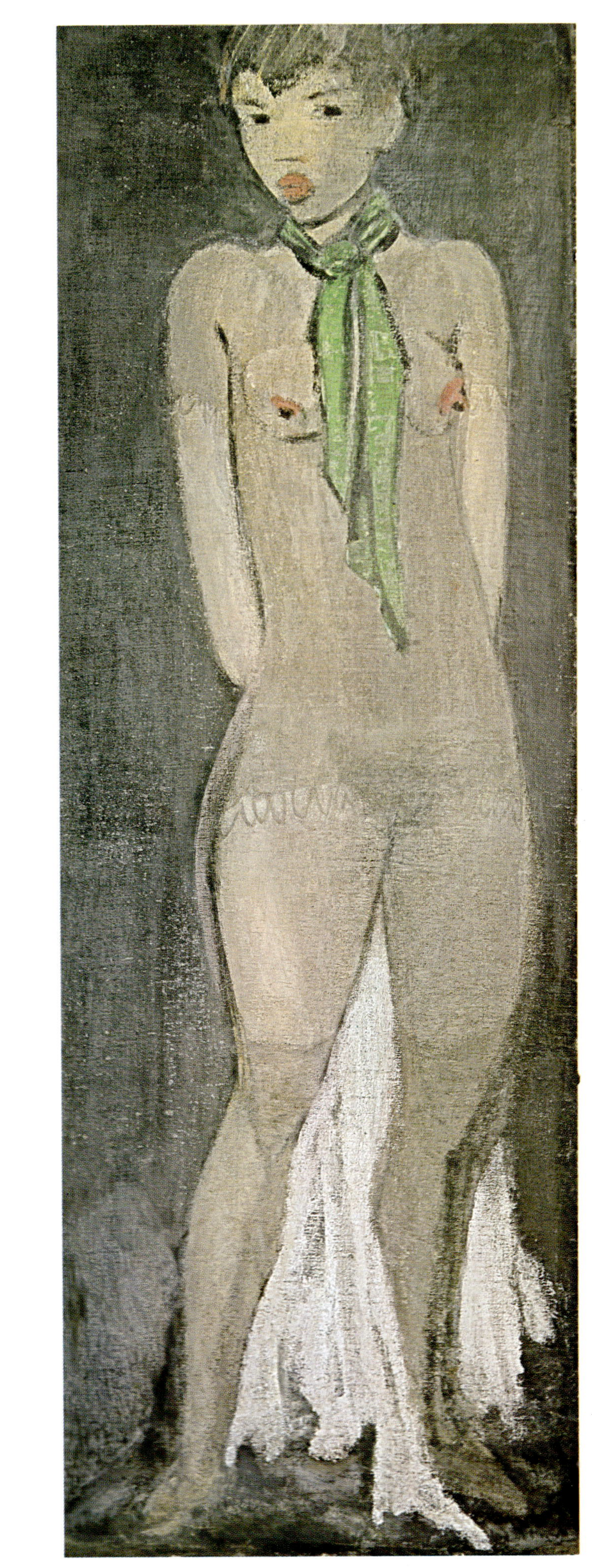

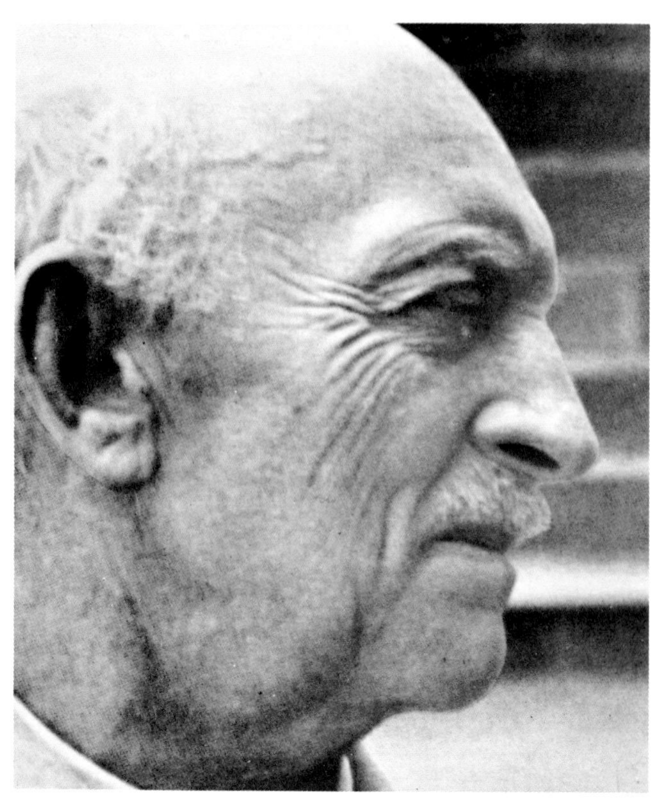

# Emil Nolde

NOLDE 1867 - 1956 SEEBUELL

51 South Sea Islander
Watercolor, 1914
18⅜ x 13¾″ (46.7 x 35 cm)
Signed lower right

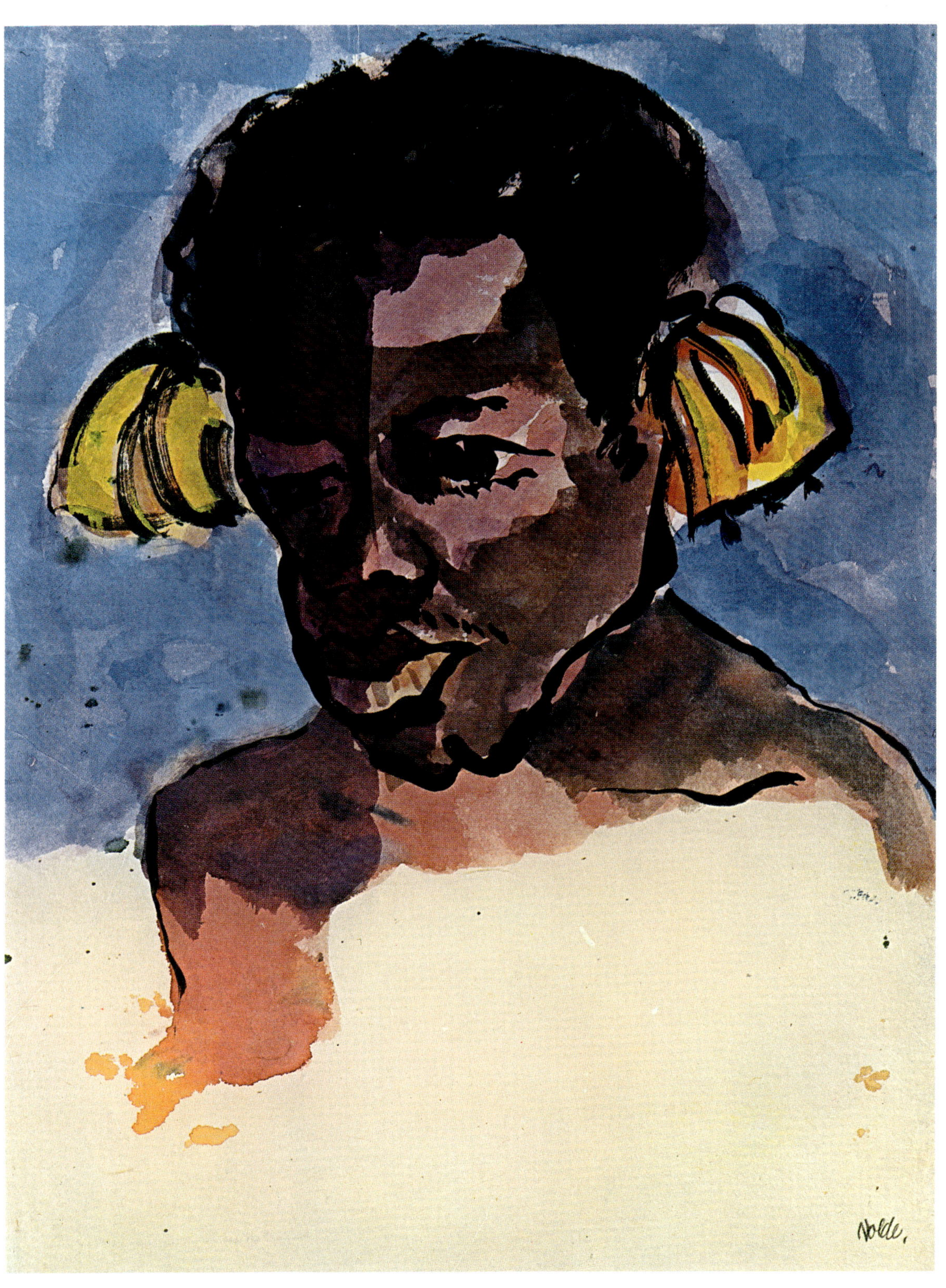

# Emil Nolde

52 **South Sea Landscape with Native Hut**
Watercolor, 1914
13¾ x 19⅛″ (35 x 48.6 cm)
Signed lower right

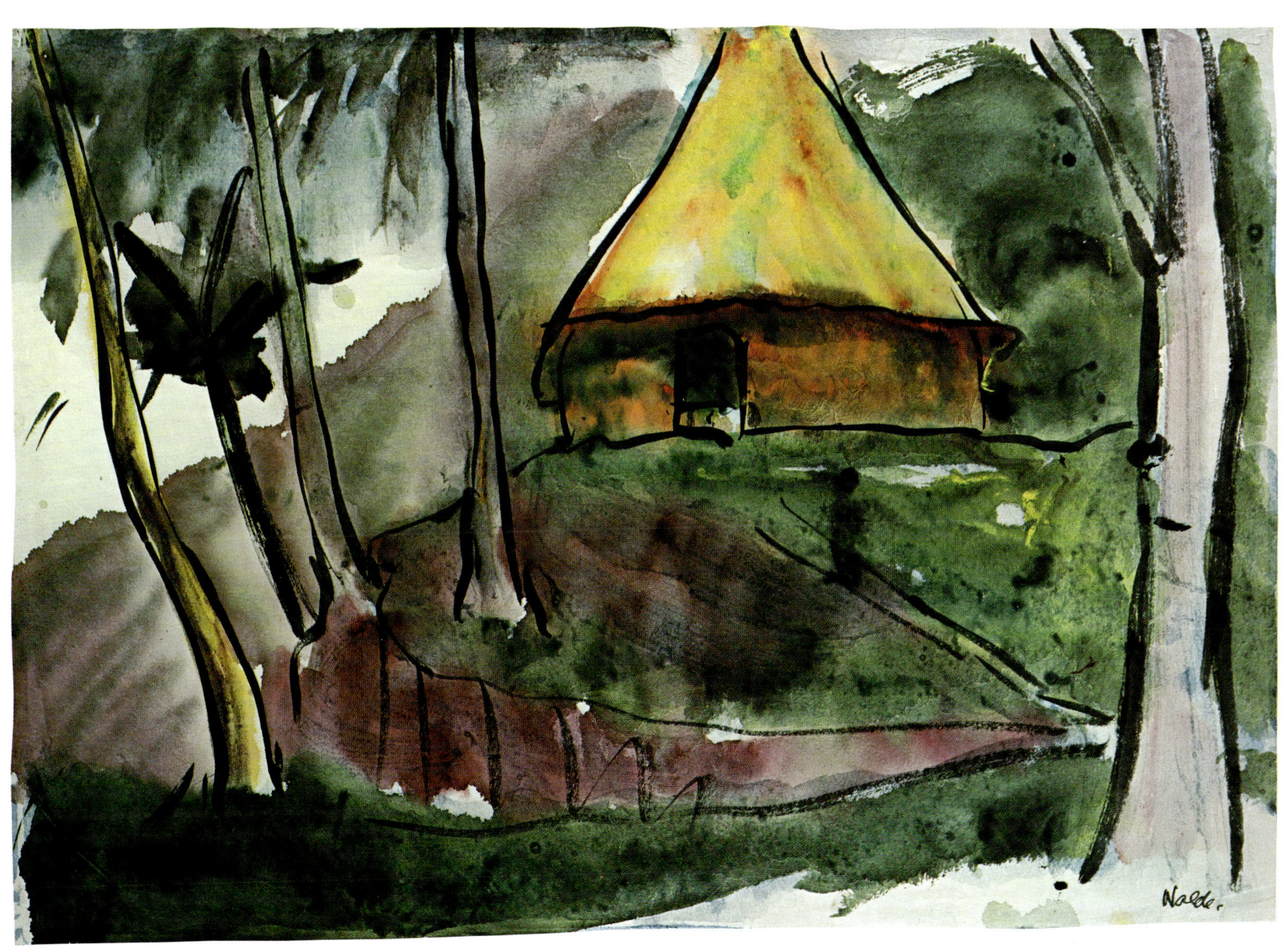

Nolde.

Emil Nolde

53  Ingeborg
Oil on canvas, 1919
16¼ x 10¾″ (41.3 x 27.3 cm)
Signed lower left

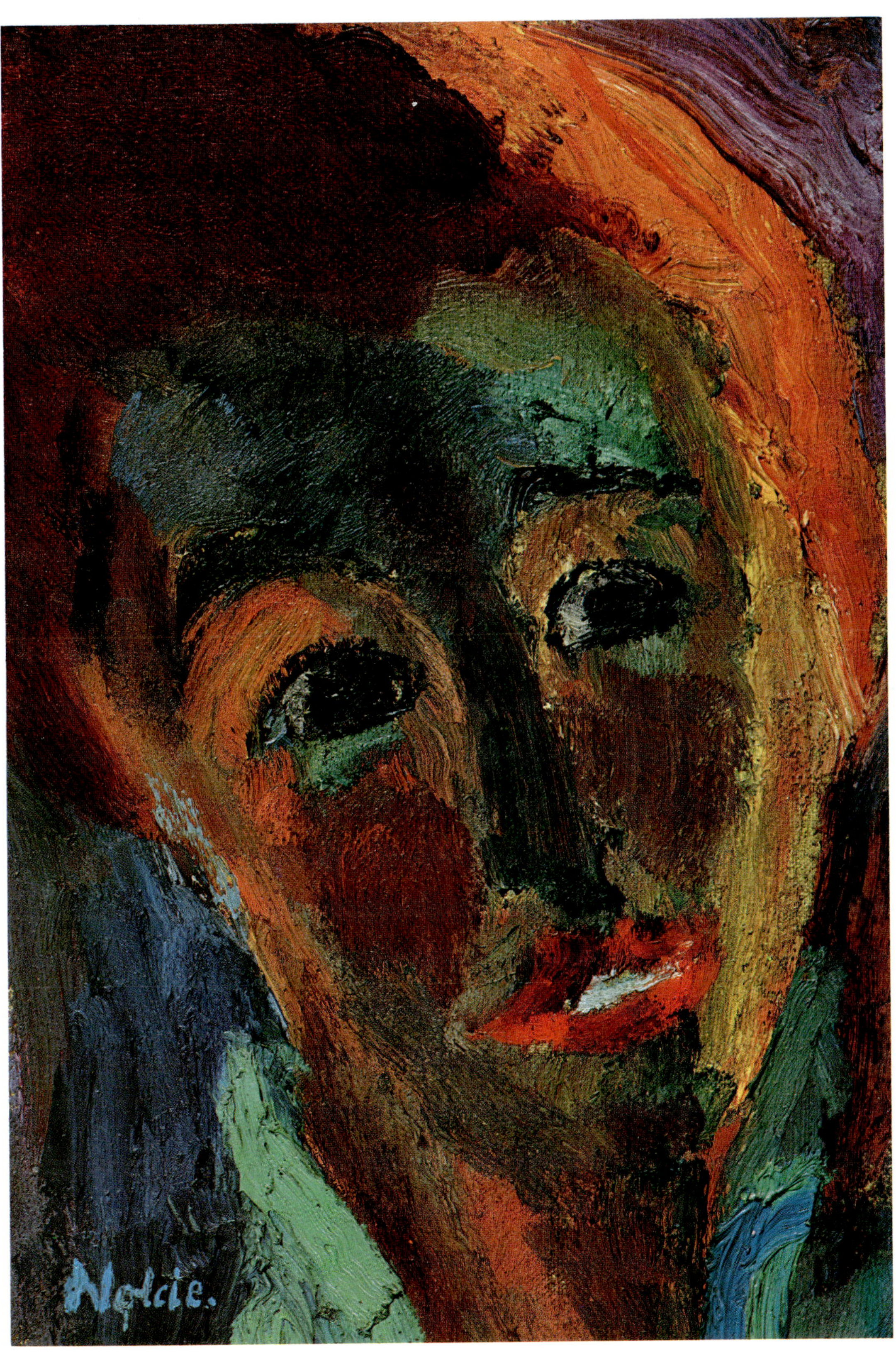

# Emil Nolde

54 Marsh Landscape
Watercolor
13½ x 18½″ (34.3 x 47 cm)
Signed lower right

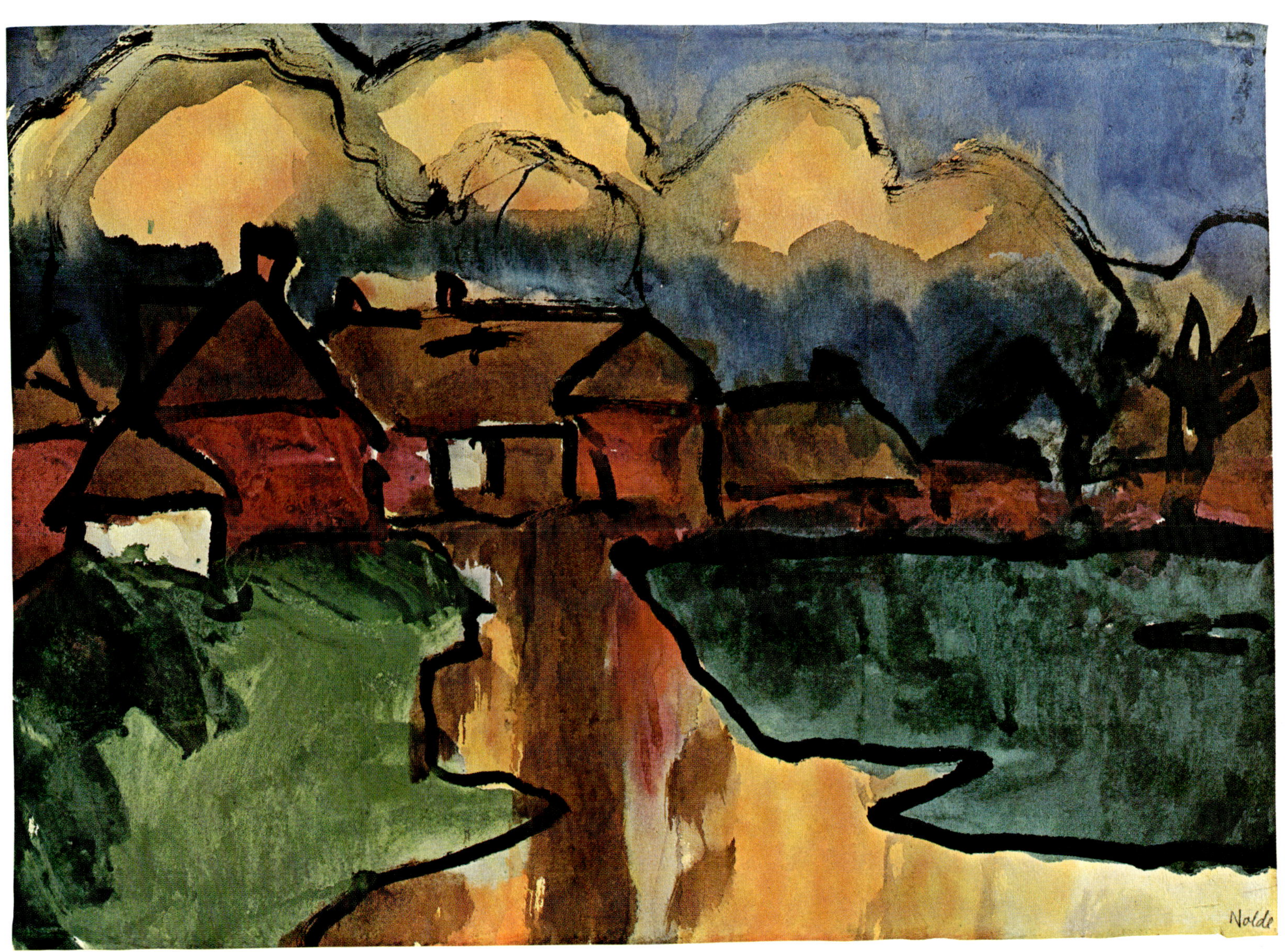

# Emil Nolde

55   **Red Poppies**
Watercolor
13¾ x 18¾″ (35 x 47.6 cm)
Signed lower left

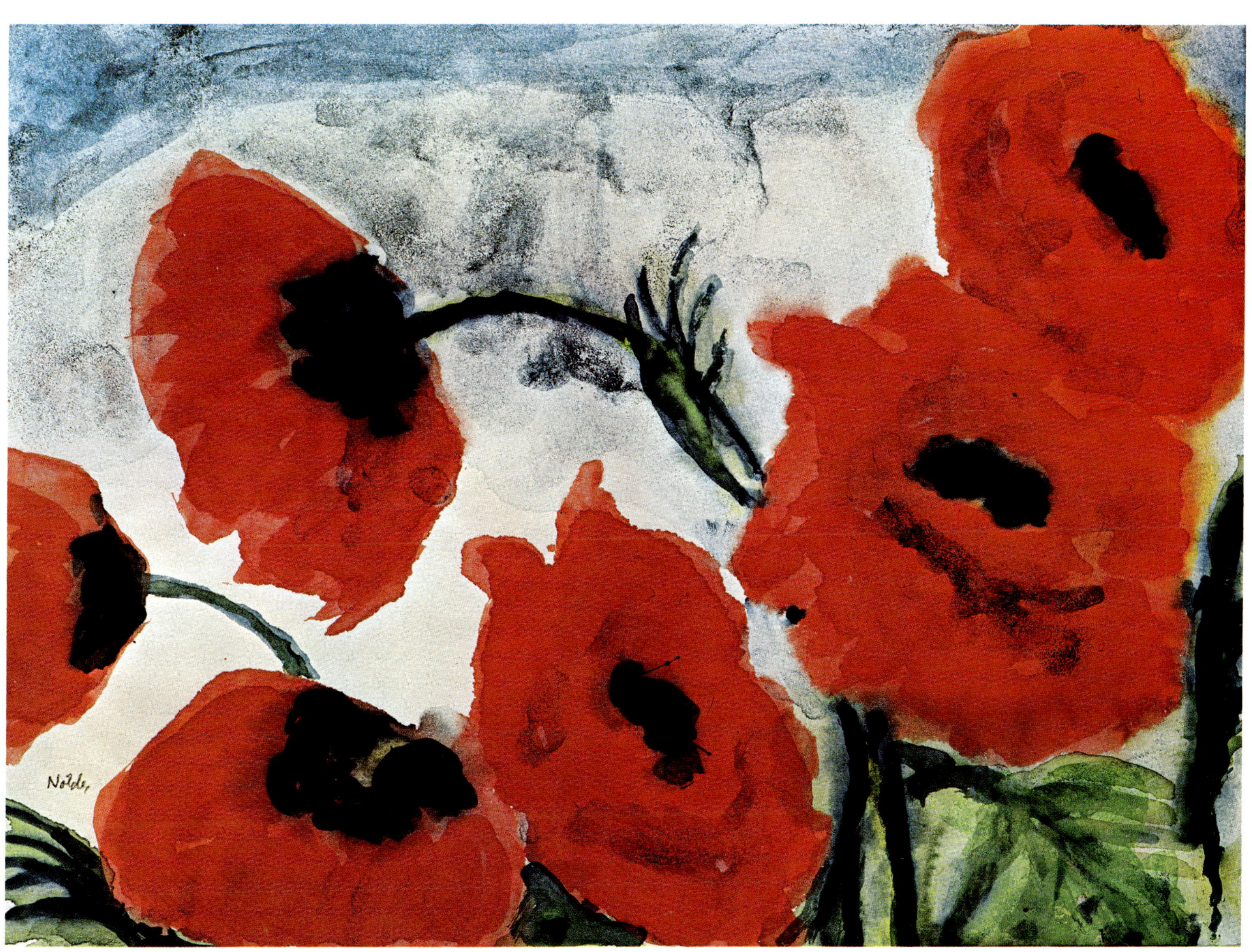

Emil Nolde

56 Chameleons
Watercolor
13⅞ x 18⅝″ (35.3 x 47.3 cm)
Signed lower right

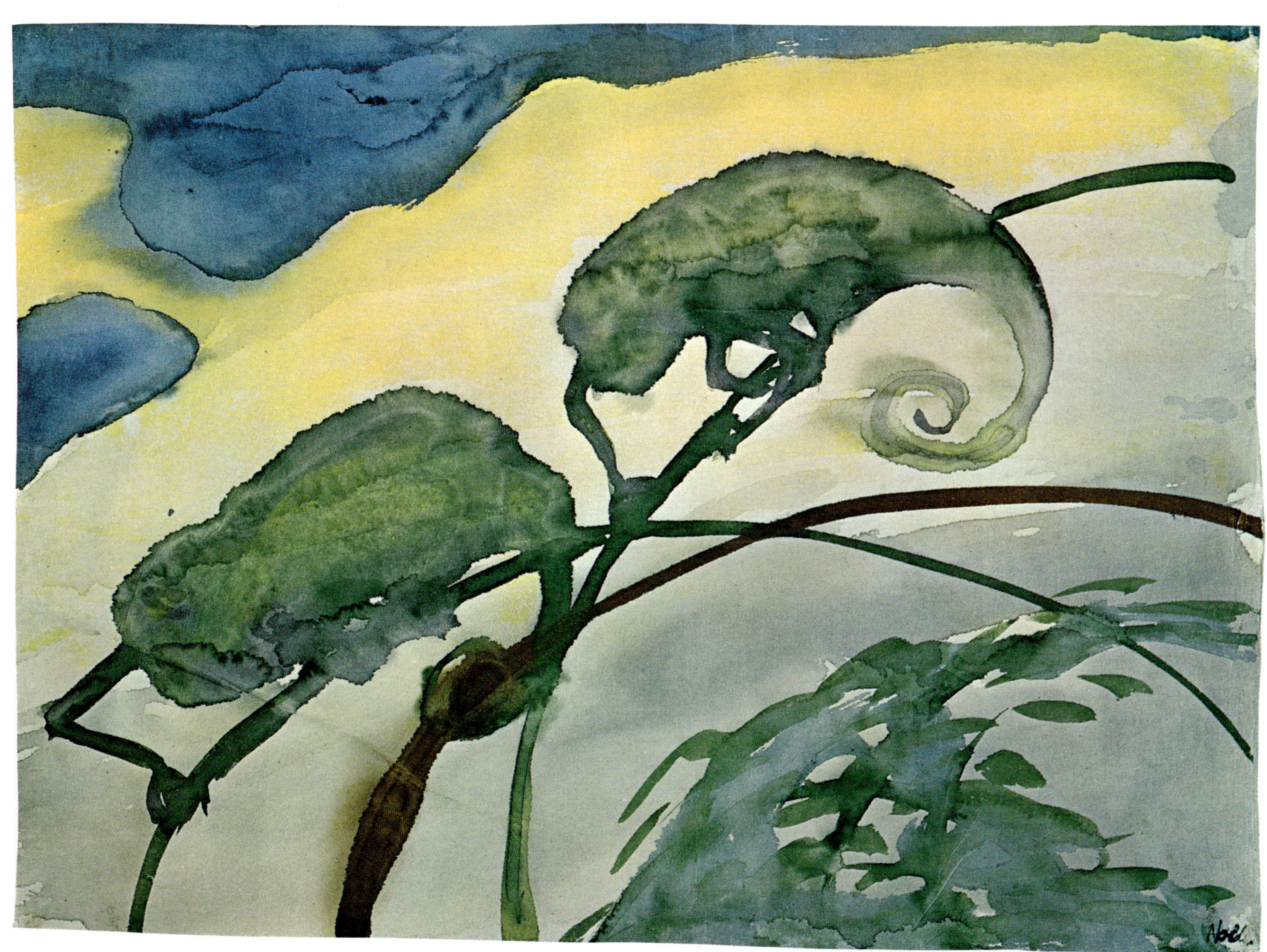

# Emil Nolde

57  Romantic Landscape
Watercolor
6¾ x 6¾″ (17.1 x 17.1 cm)
Signed lower right

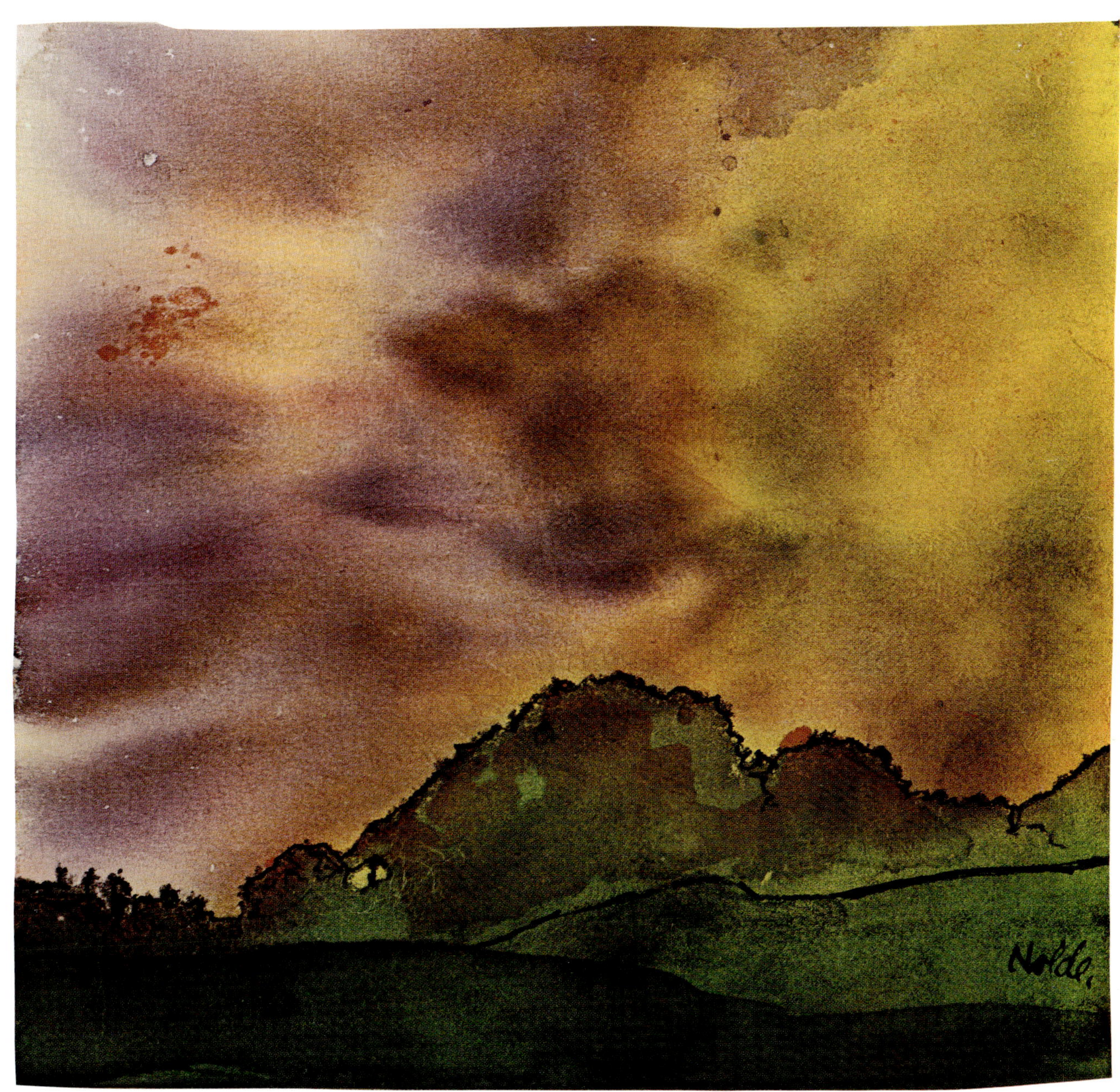
Nolde.

# Emil Nolde

58  Flower Stillife
Watercolor
13¾ x 18½″ (35 x 47 cm)
Signed center right

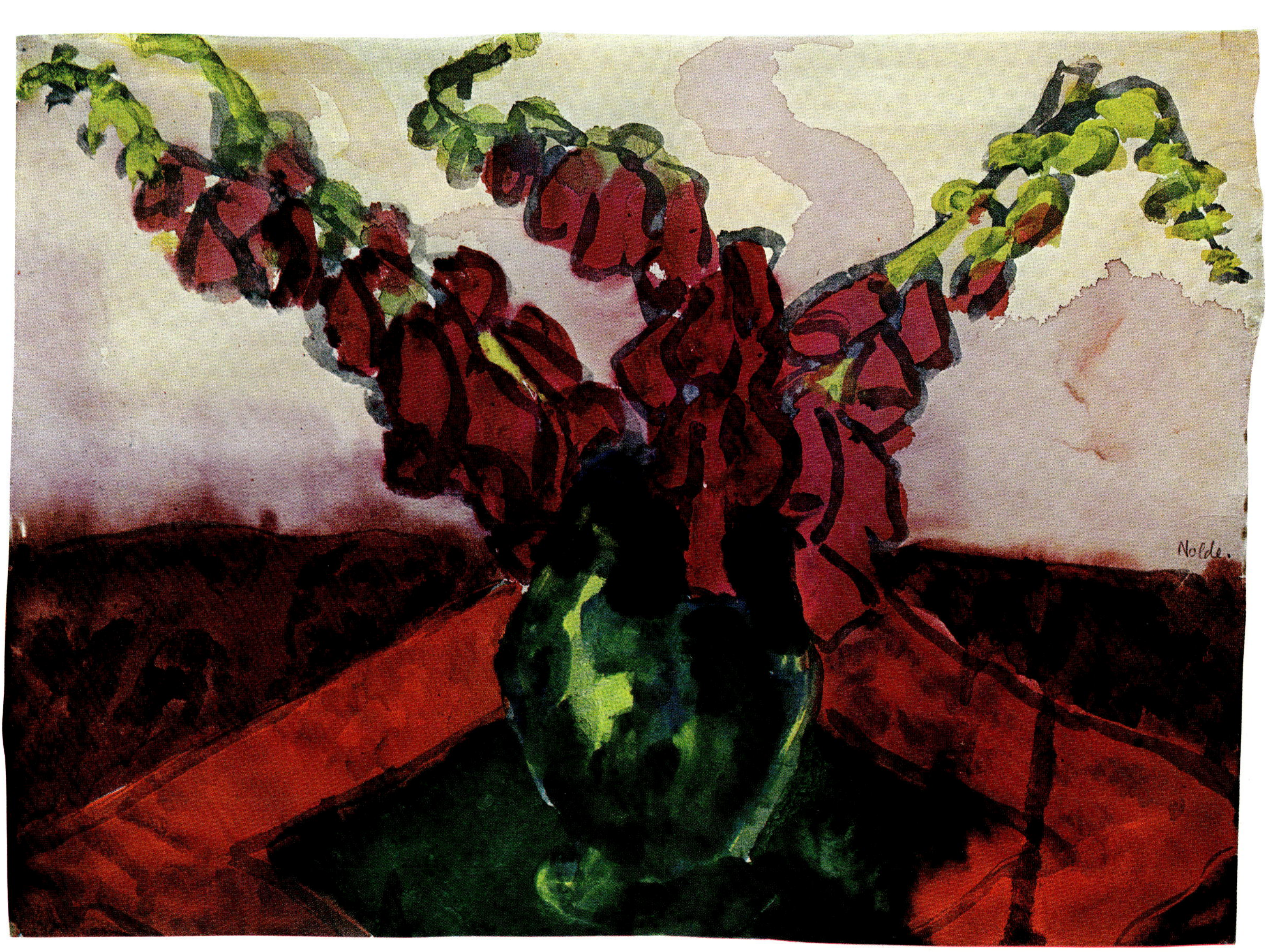

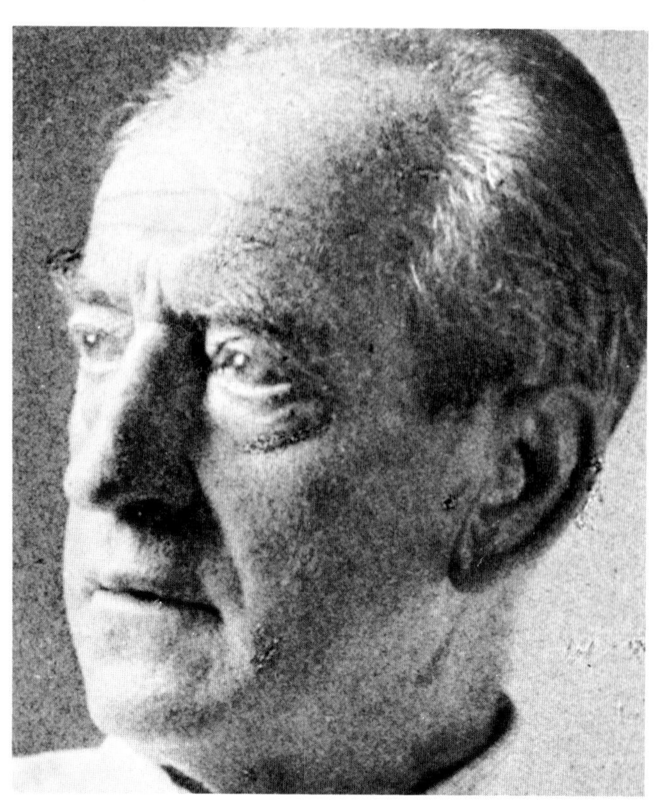

# Max Pechstein

ZWICKAU 1881 - 1955 BERLIN

59 Fisherman
Oil on board, 1910-13
21½ x 18″ (54.6 x 45.7 cm)
Signed lower left

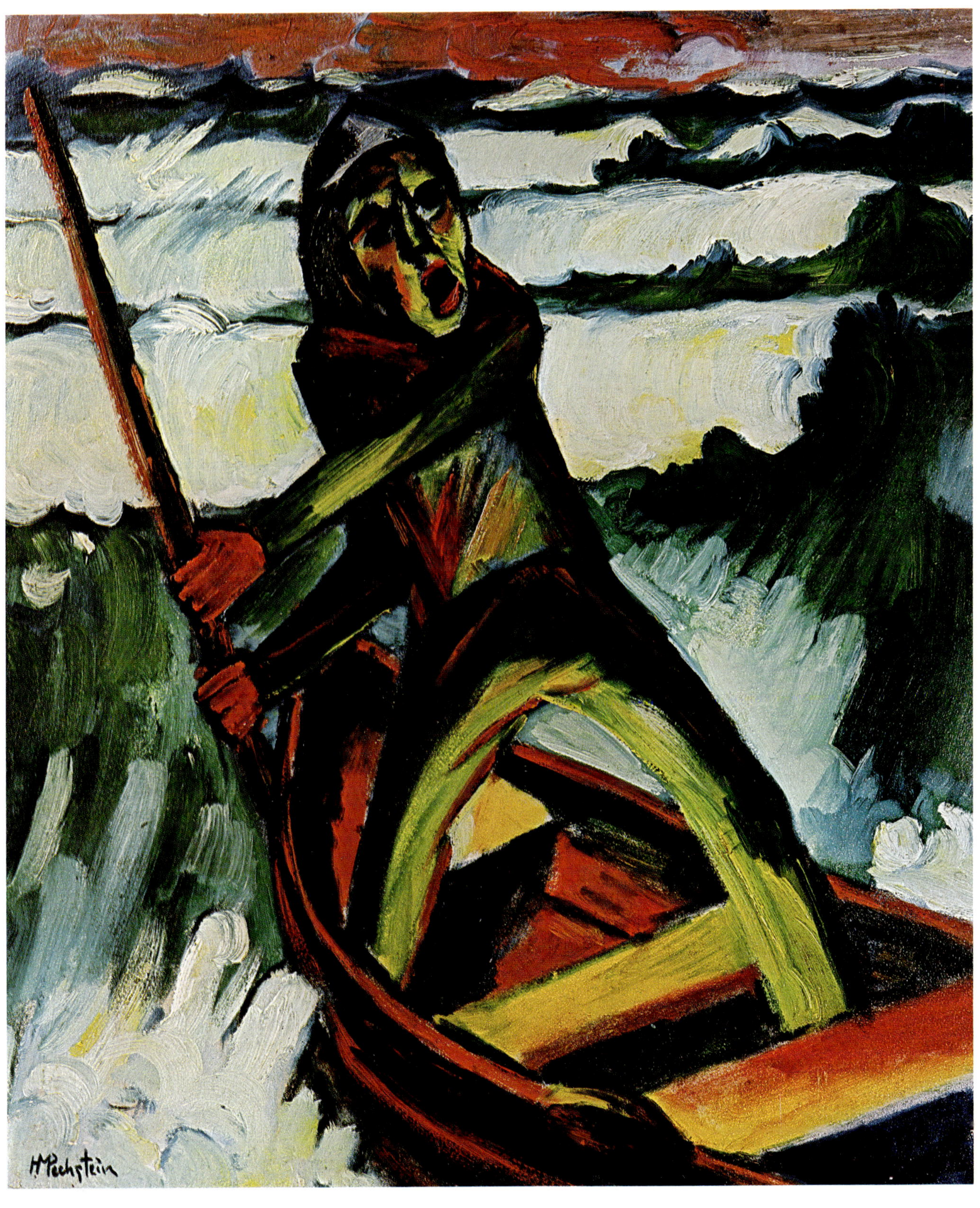

HPechstein

# Max Pechstein

**60**   **Zwei Akte am Waldesrand**
*(Two Nudes in Forest)*
Oil on canvas, 1912
39 x 27⅝" (99.1 x 70.2 cm)
Initialed and dated lower left

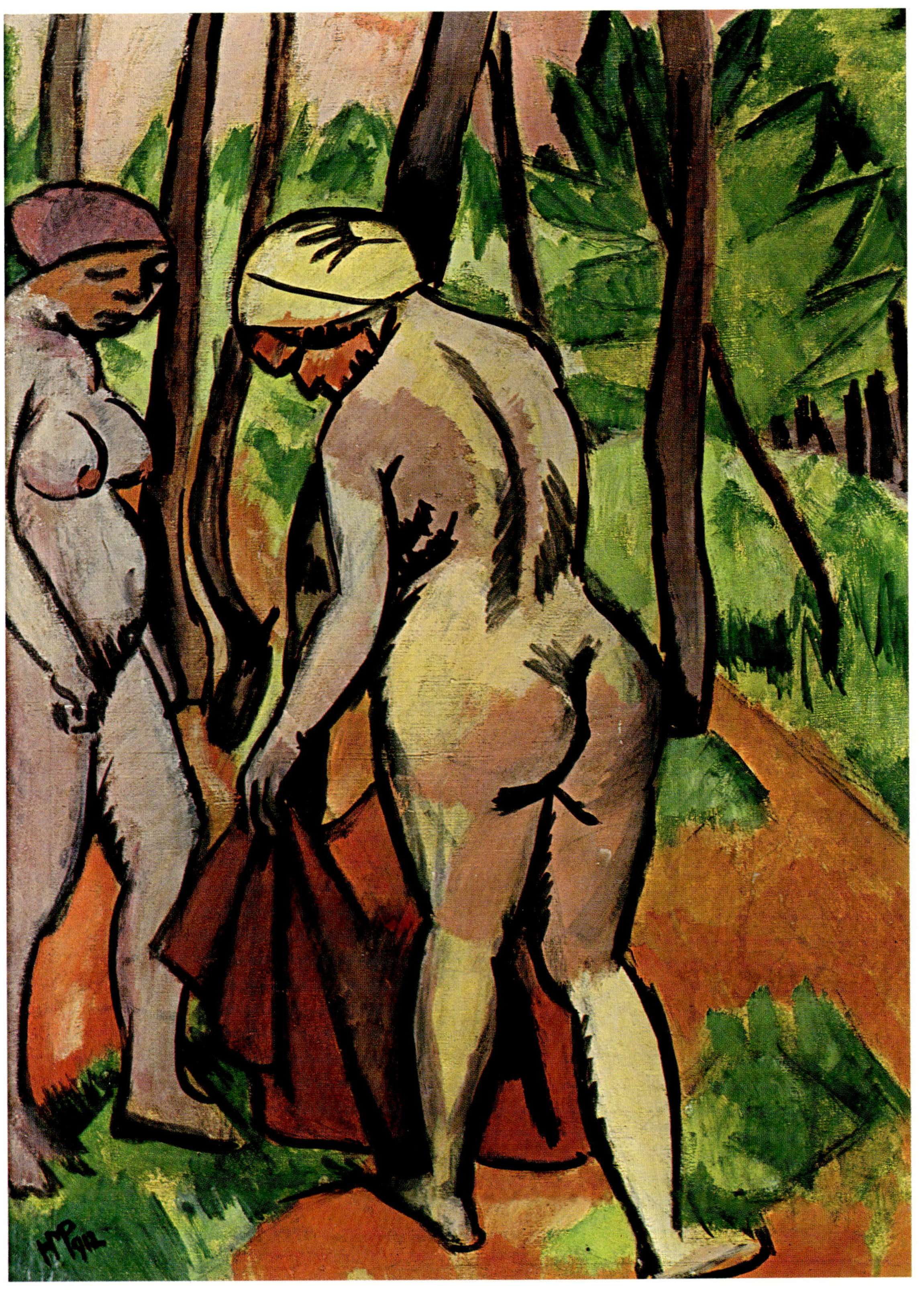

# Max Pechstein

**60** REVERSE

**Stillife
with Flowering Plant**
Oil on canvas, 1913
39 x 27⅝″ (99.1 x 70.2 cm)
Initialed and dated lower right

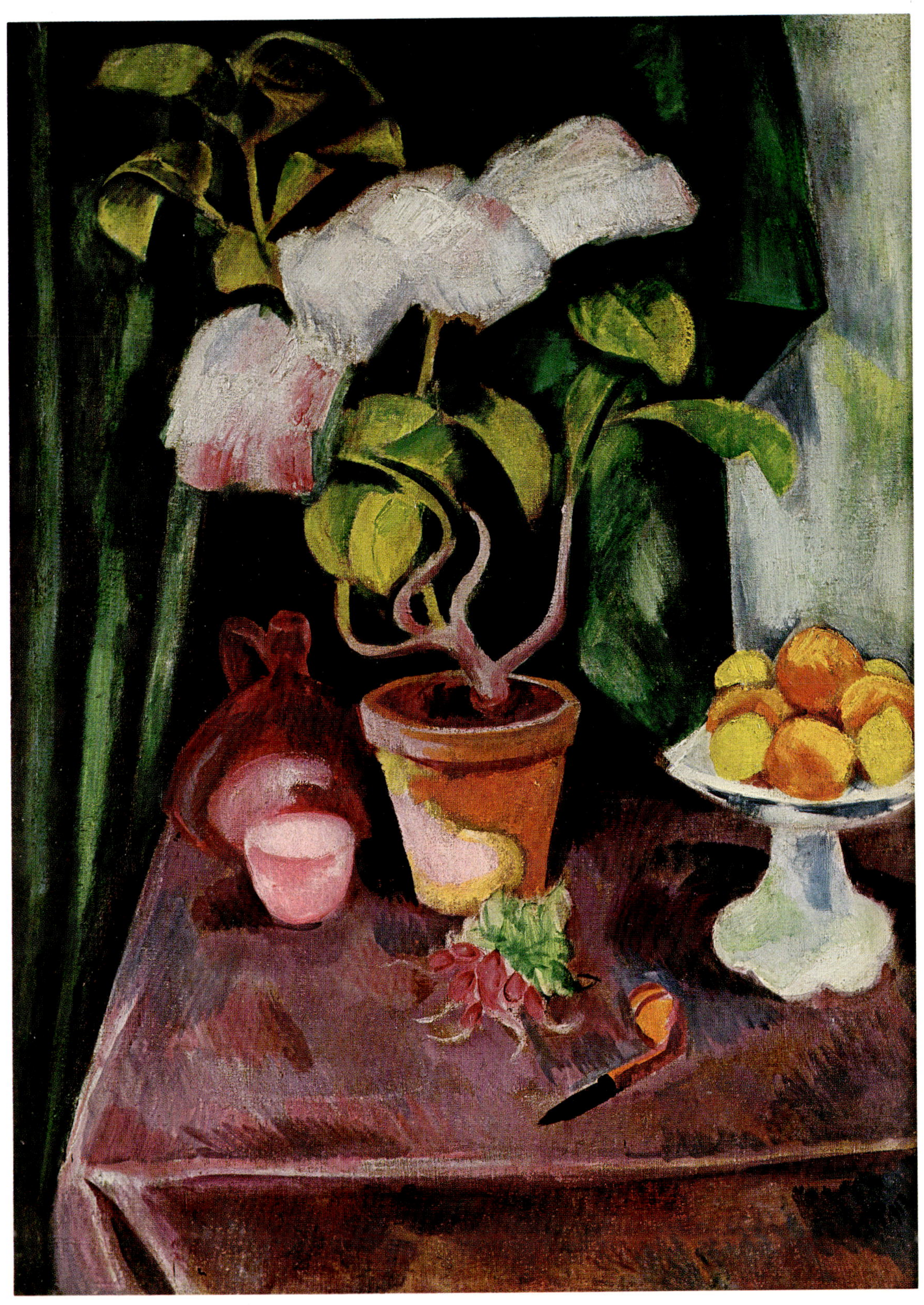

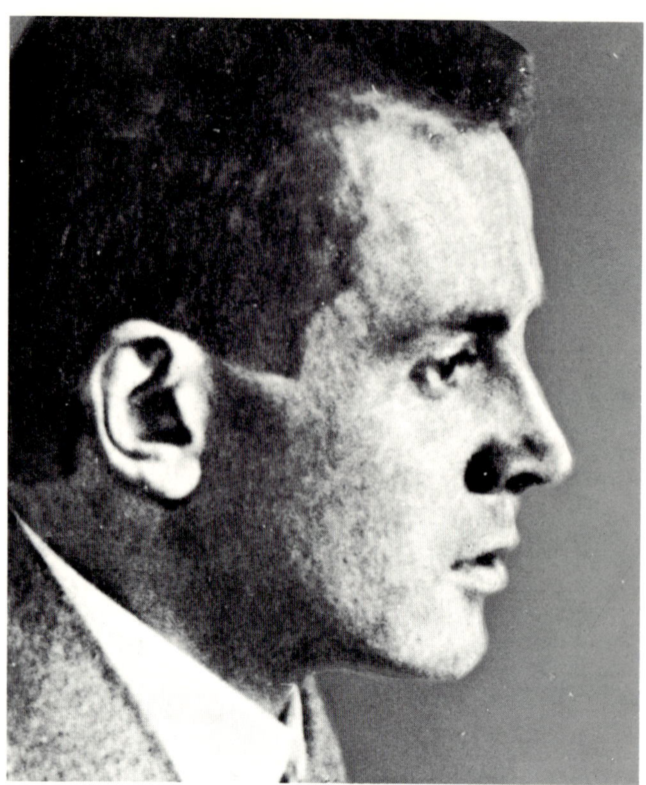

# Egon Schiele

TULLN 1890 - 1918 VIENNA

**61** Kneeling Girl with Raised Arms
Crayon, watercolor and gouache, 1910
17¼ x 11¾" (43.8 x 29.8 cm)
Signed and dated lower right

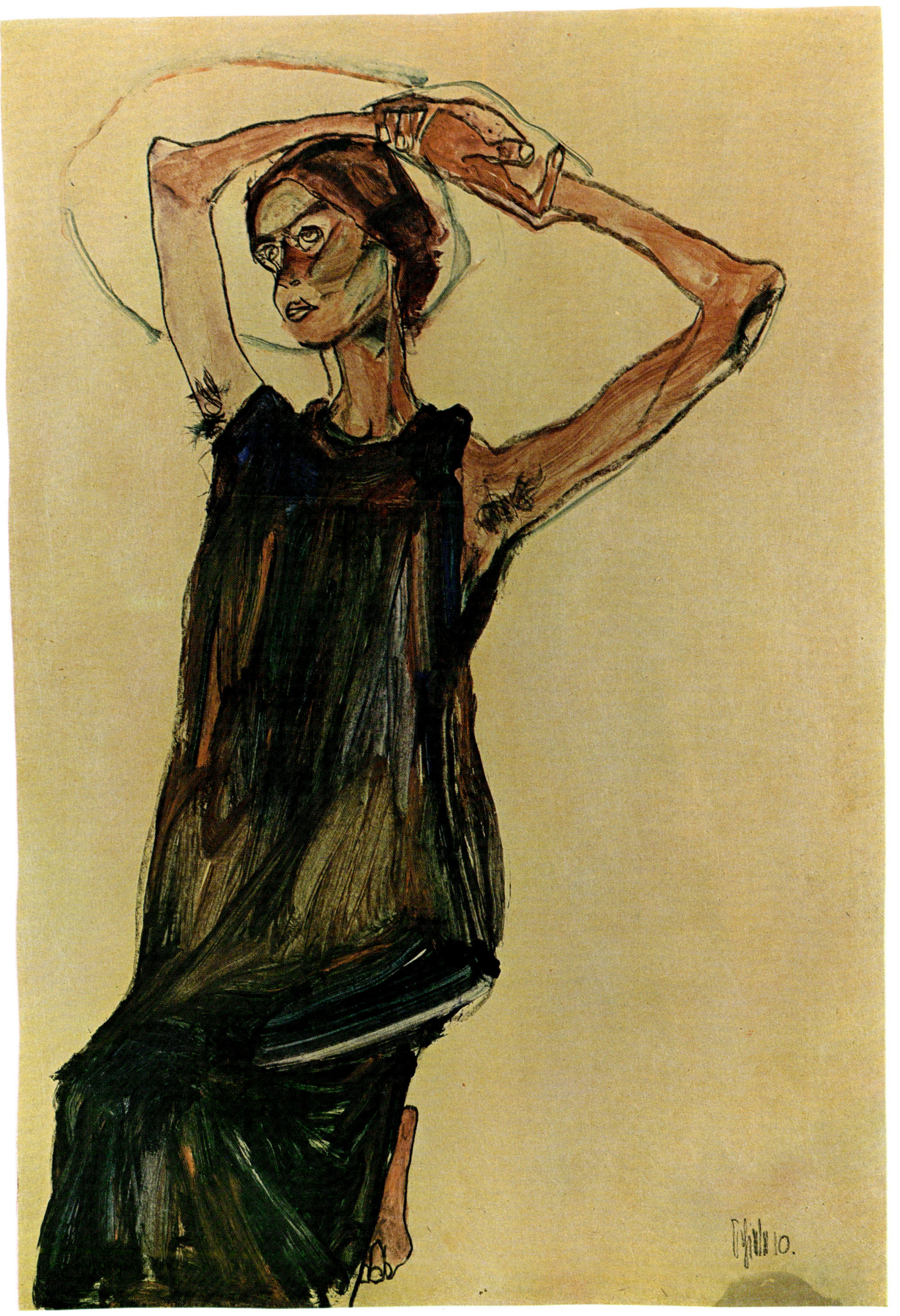
Schiele 10.

# Egon Schiele

62   **Weiblicher Rueckenakt**
*(Female Nude seen from the back)*
Oil on canvas, 1913
75½ x 20¾″ (192 x 52.7 cm)

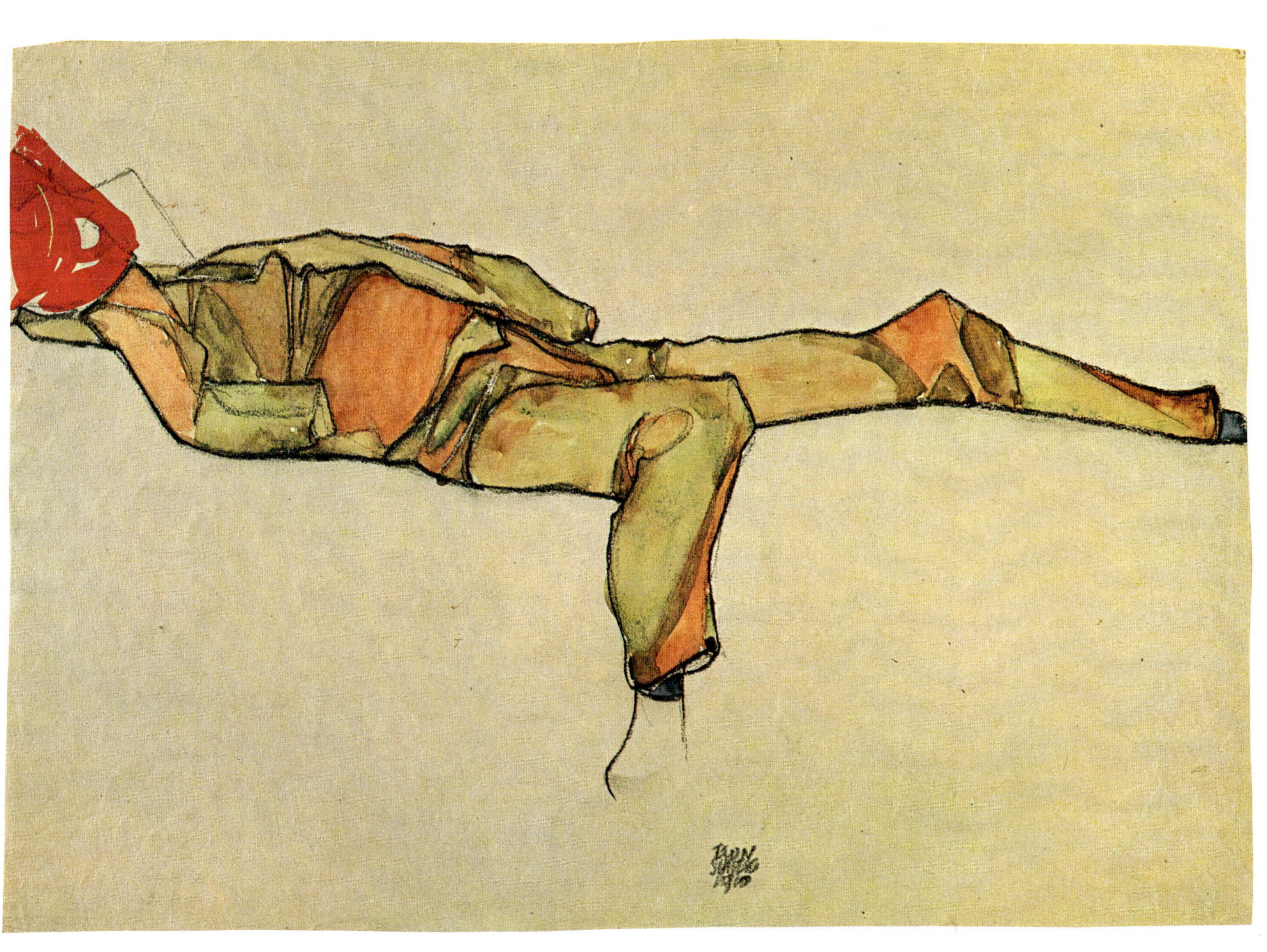

# Egon Schiele

64   **Portrait of Oskar Reichel**
Pencil, watercolor and gouache, 1910
17⅝ x 12¼″ (44.8 x 31.1 cm)
Initialed and dated center right
Titled center left

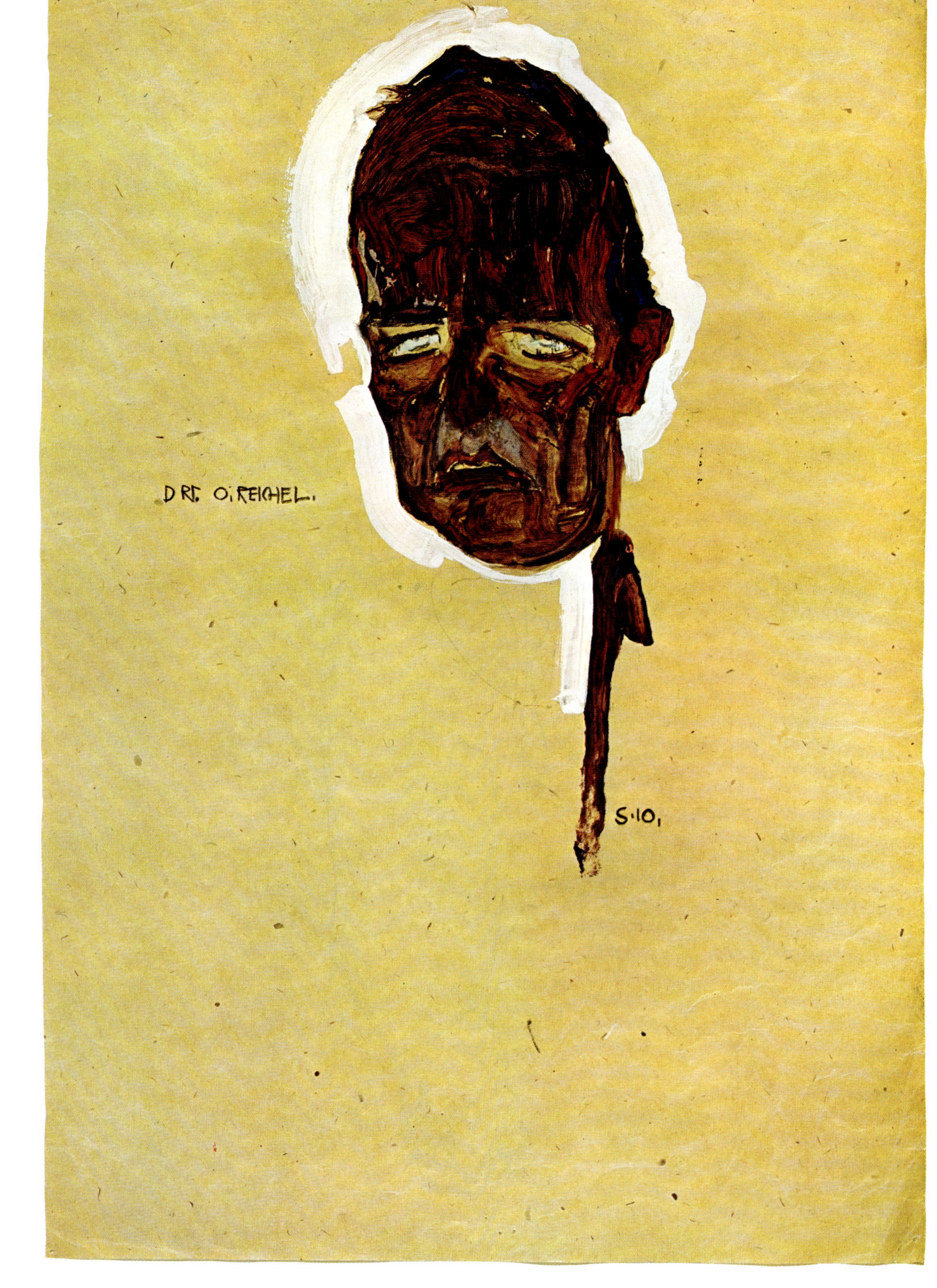

DR. O, REICHEL.
S·10·

Egon Schiele

65 **Sleeping Nude**
Pencil and watercolor, 1913
19⅛ x 12⅝″ (48.6 x 32 cm)
Signed and dated lower left
Reverse: Reclining Male Nude
Pencil

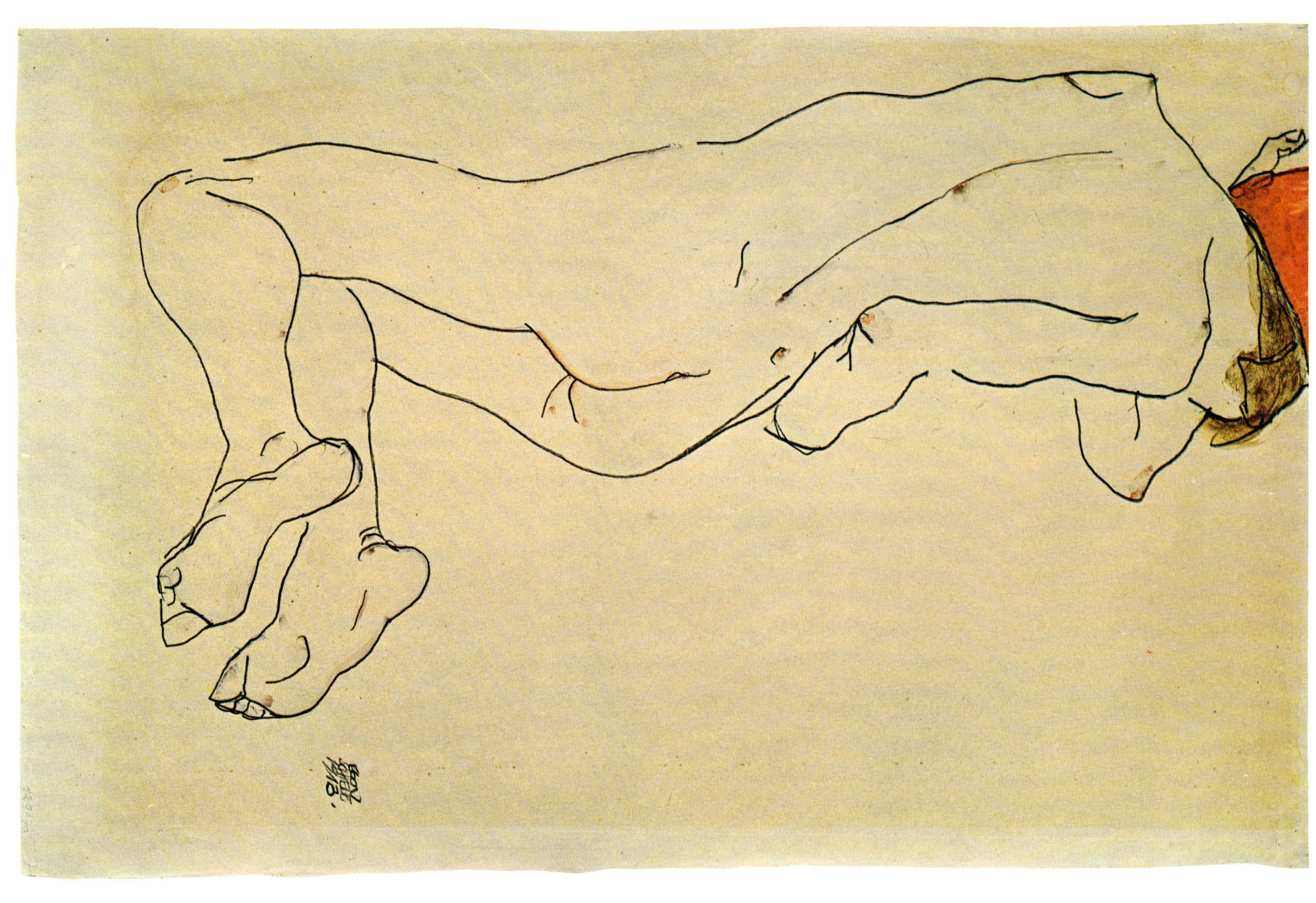

# Egon Schiele

66 Schwestern (Sisters)
Pencil and watercolor, 1913
19 x 12½″ (48.2 x 31.7 cm)
Signed and dated lower right
Titled lower center
Estate stamp on reverse

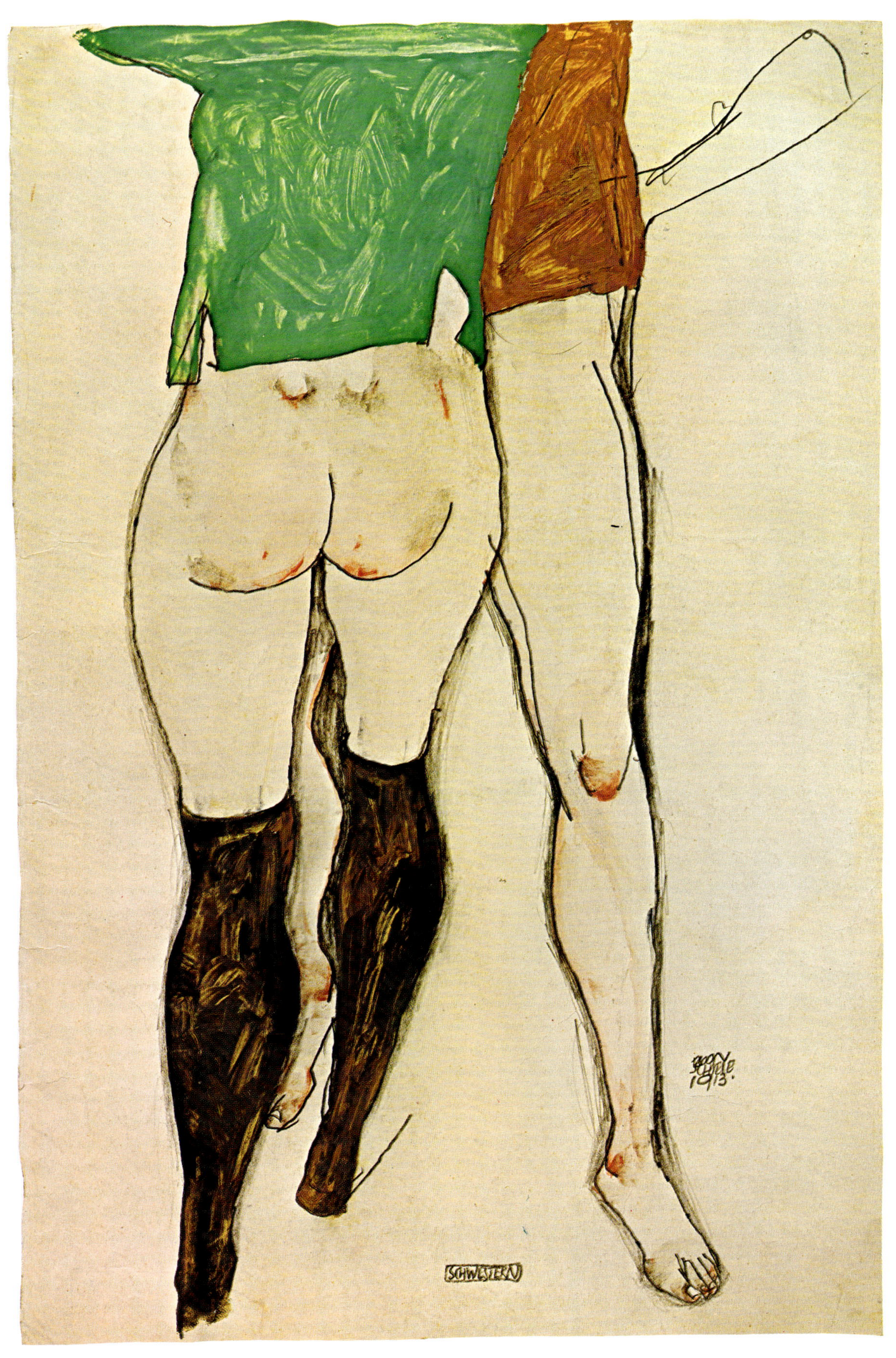

EGON SCHIELE
1913
SCHWESTERN

# Egon Schiele

67 **Krumau**
Pencil, 1913
12½ x 19″ (31.7 x 48.2 cm)
Signed and dated lower right
Titled lower left
Estate stamp on reverse

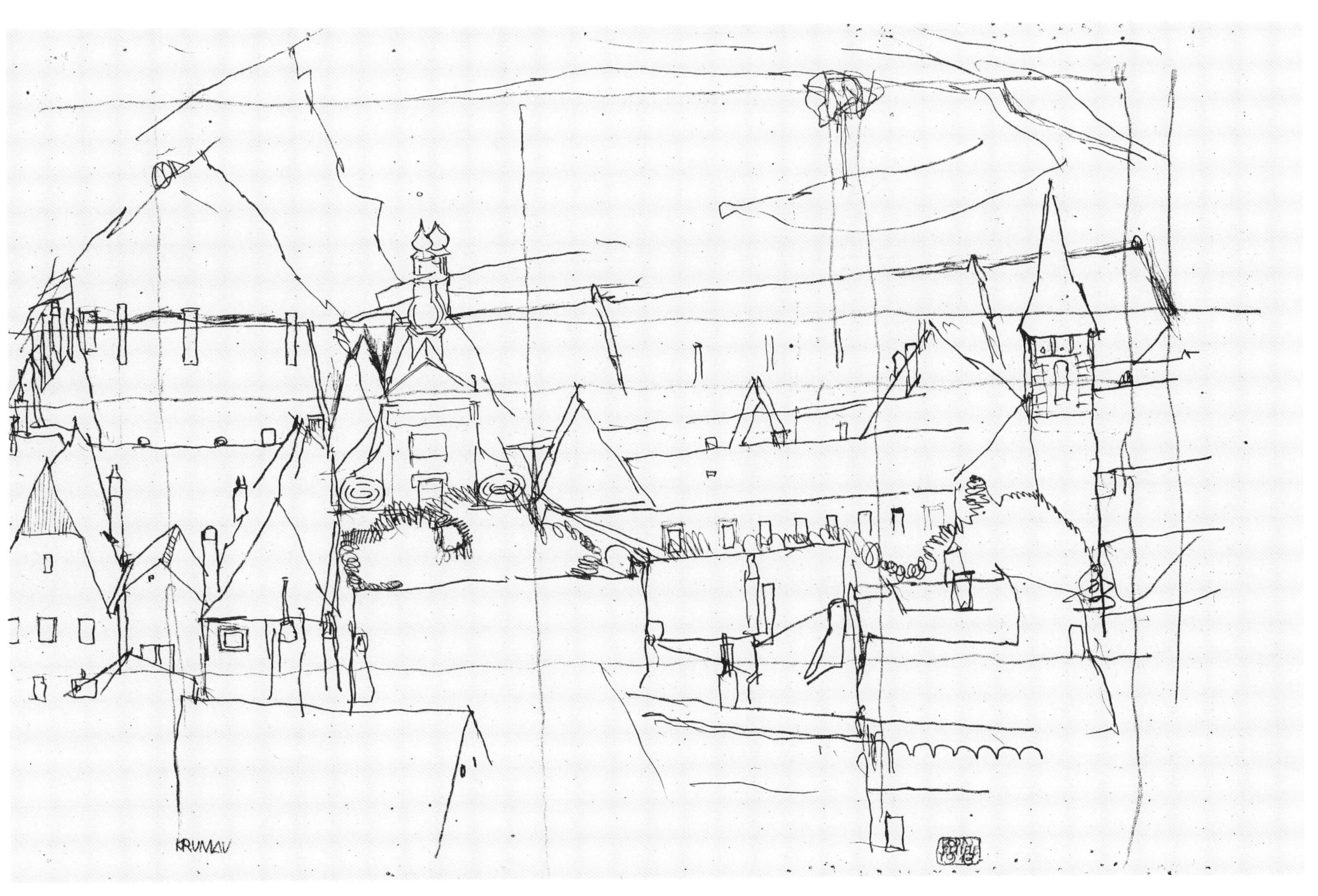
KRUMAU

# Egon Schiele

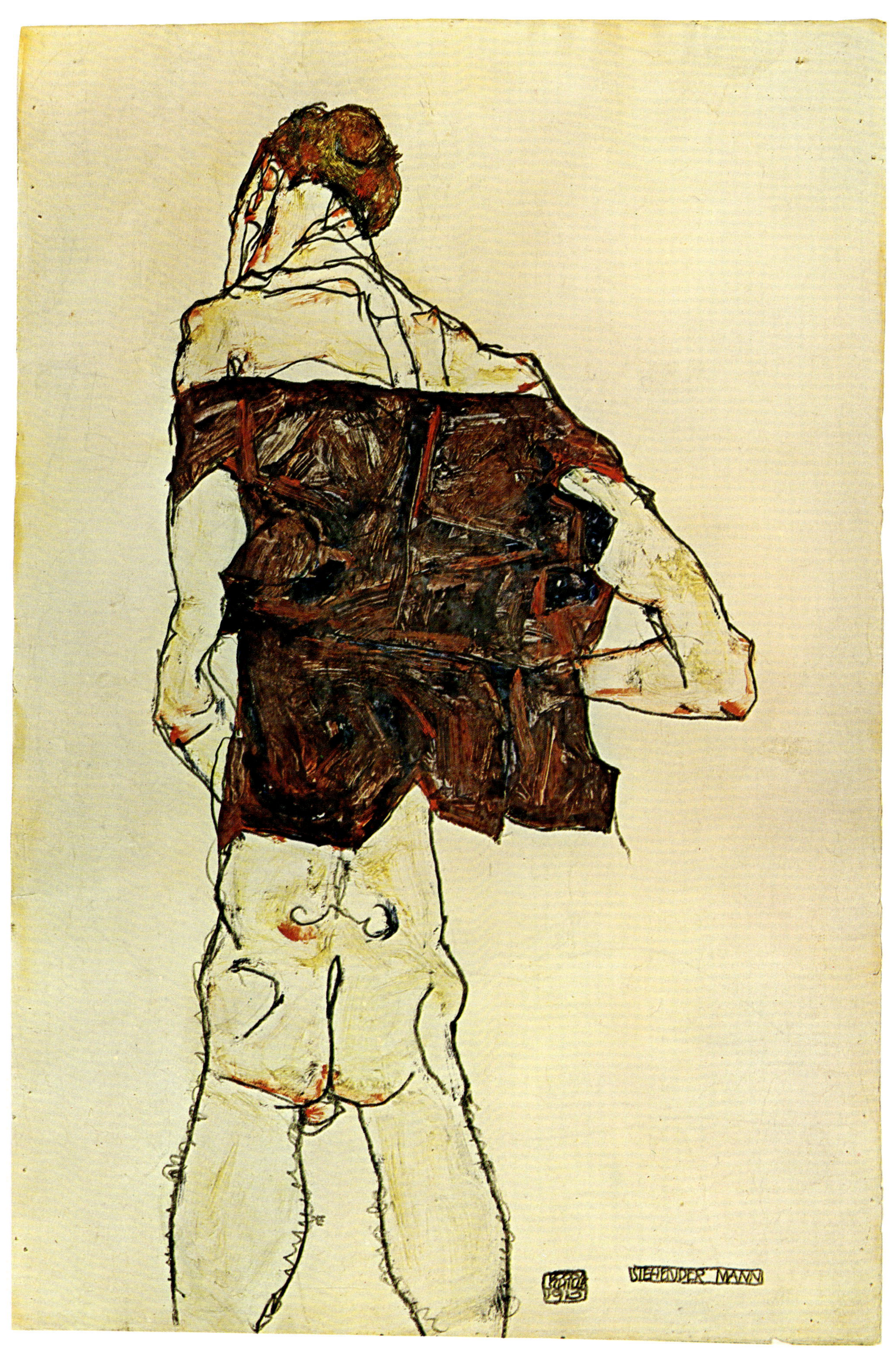

EGON
SCHIELE
1913
STEHENDER MANN

# Egon Schiele

69  Reclining Woman with Raised Skirt
Crayon, watercolor and gouache, 1914
12½ x 19″ (31.7 x 48.2 cm)
Signed and dated upper left

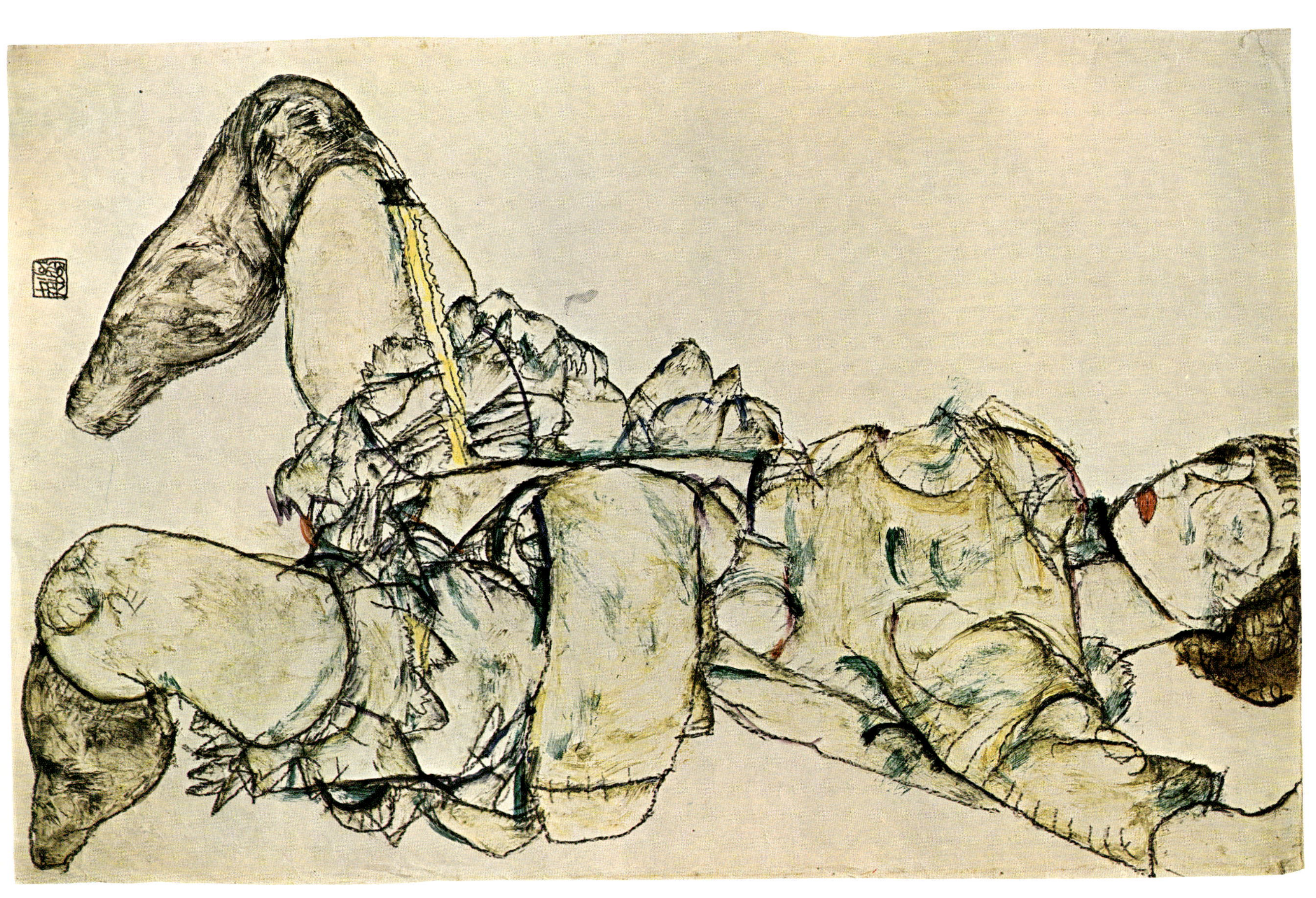

# Egon Schiele

Egon Schiele

71 Kneeling Female Nude
Black crayon, 1918
18¾ x 12½″ (47.6 x 31.7 cm)
Signed and dated lower right
Estate stamp on reverse

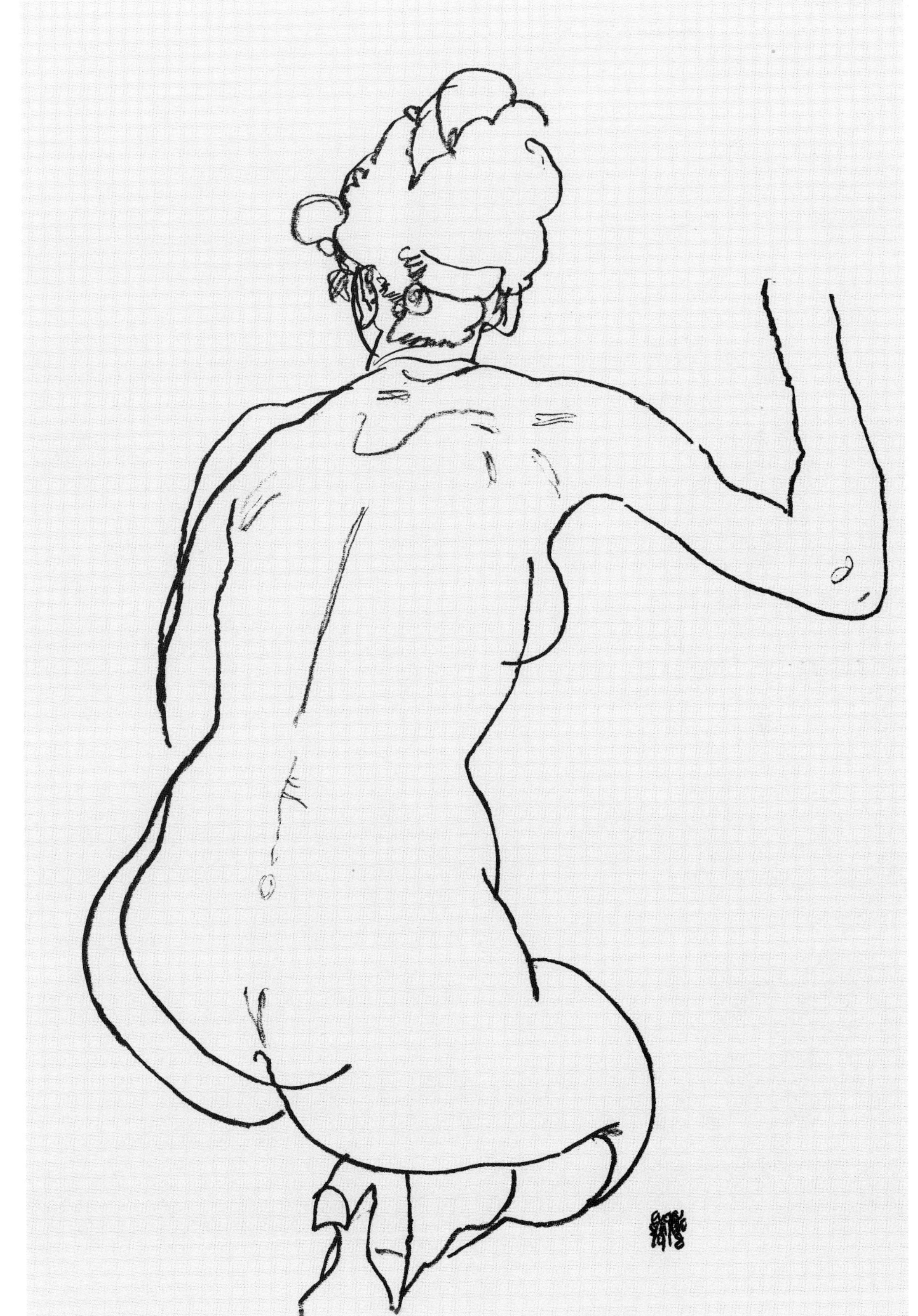

Egon Schiele

72 Crouching Nude
Charcoal, watercolor and gouache, 1918
11½ x 17⅞″ (29.2 x 45.4 cm)
Signed and dated lower left

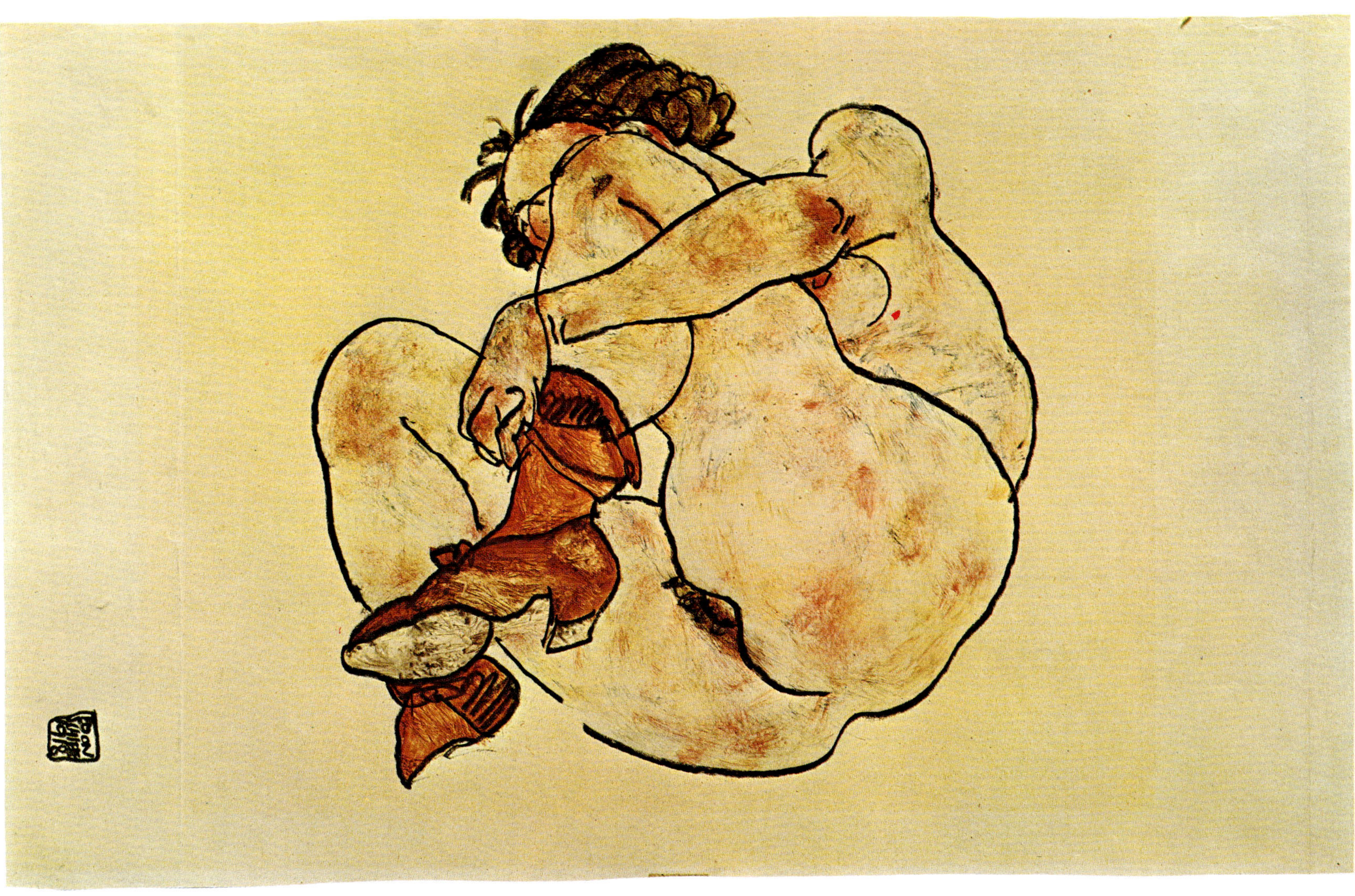

Egon Schiele

**73** Portrait of an Officer
Charcoal, 1918
17¾ x 11½″ (45 x 29.2 cm)
Signed and dated center right

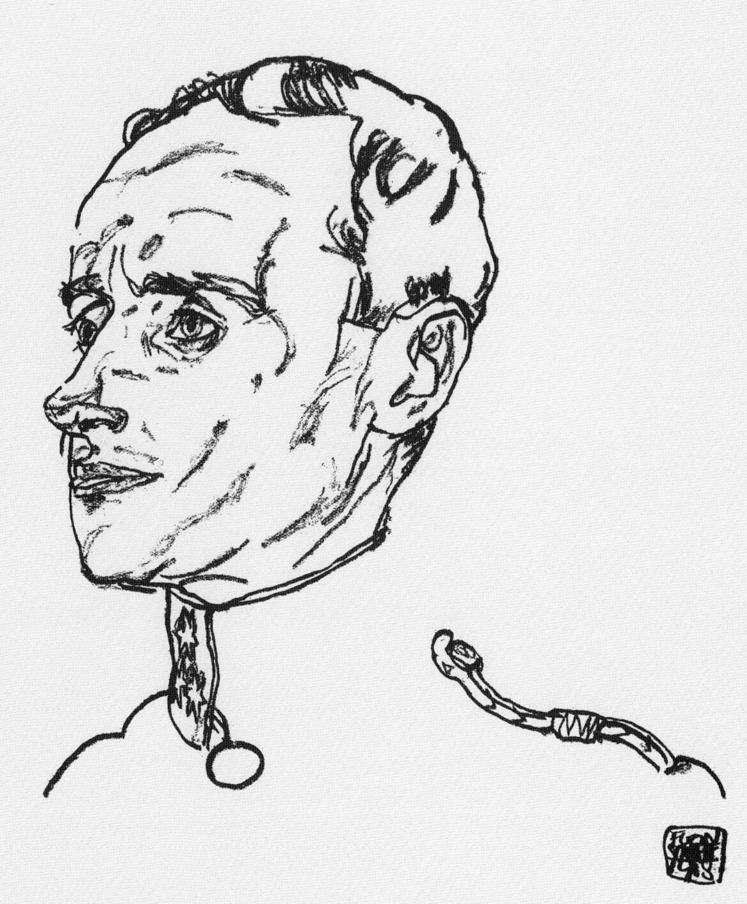

# Egon Schiele

**74** Portrait of a Woman
Watercolor and black chalk, 1918
17⅜ x 11⅝″ (44.1 x 28.9 cm)
Signed and dated lower right

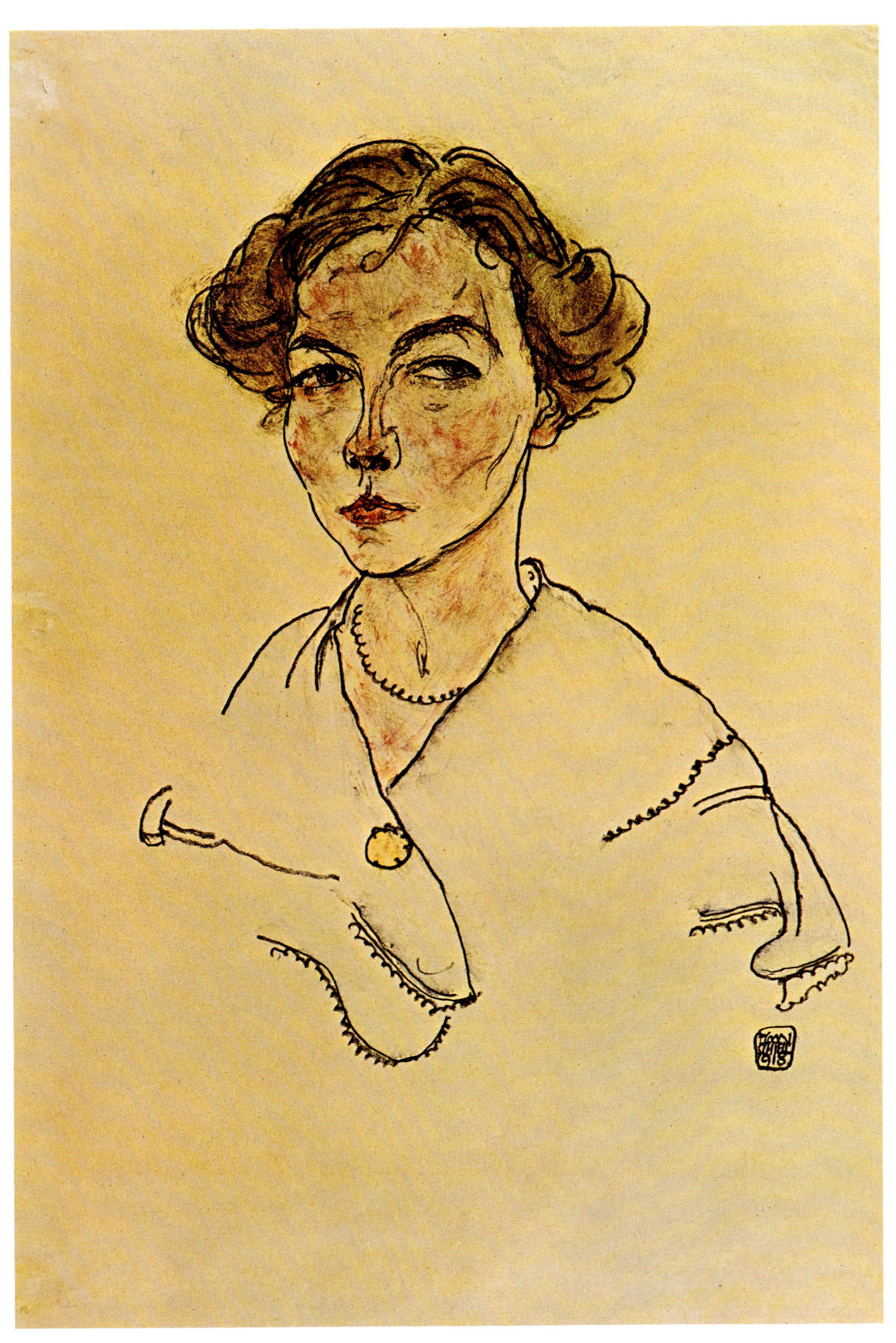

Egon Schiele

75 **Flower Studies**
Crayon and watercolor, 1918
18⅜ x 11⅞″ (46.7 x 30.2 cm)
Estate stamp lower left

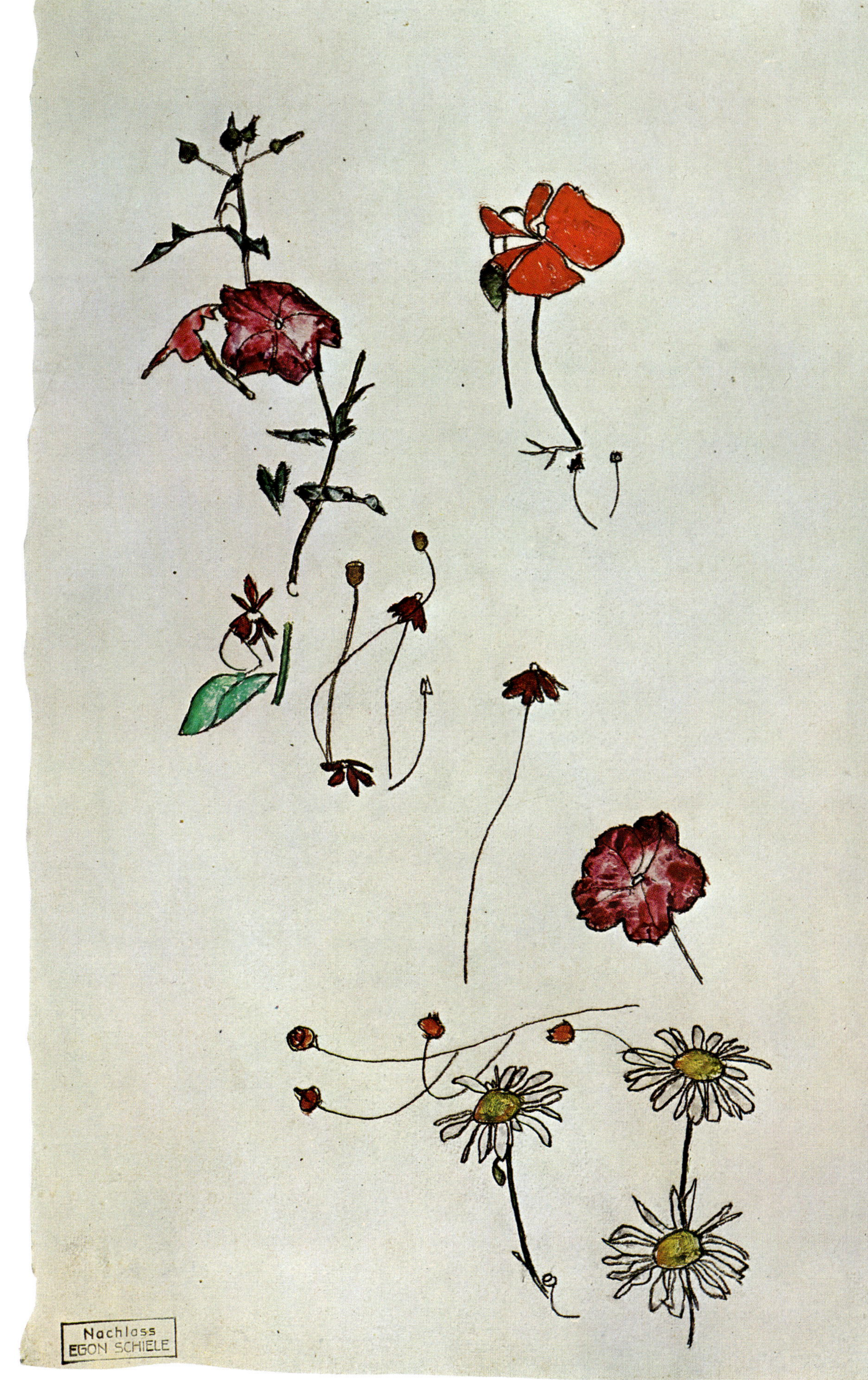
Nachlass
EGON SCHIELE

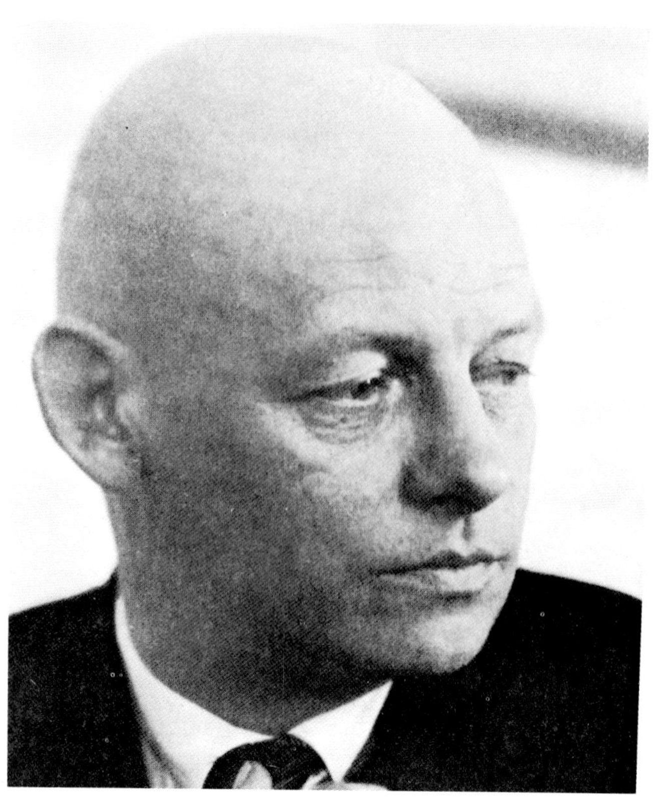

# Oskar Schlemmer

STUTTGART 1888 - 1943 BADEN-BADEN

76 Bauplastik R
*(Constructive Sculpture R)*
Aluminium, 1919
43¼ x 13¾″ (109.9 x 35 cm)
One of seven casts started in 1959

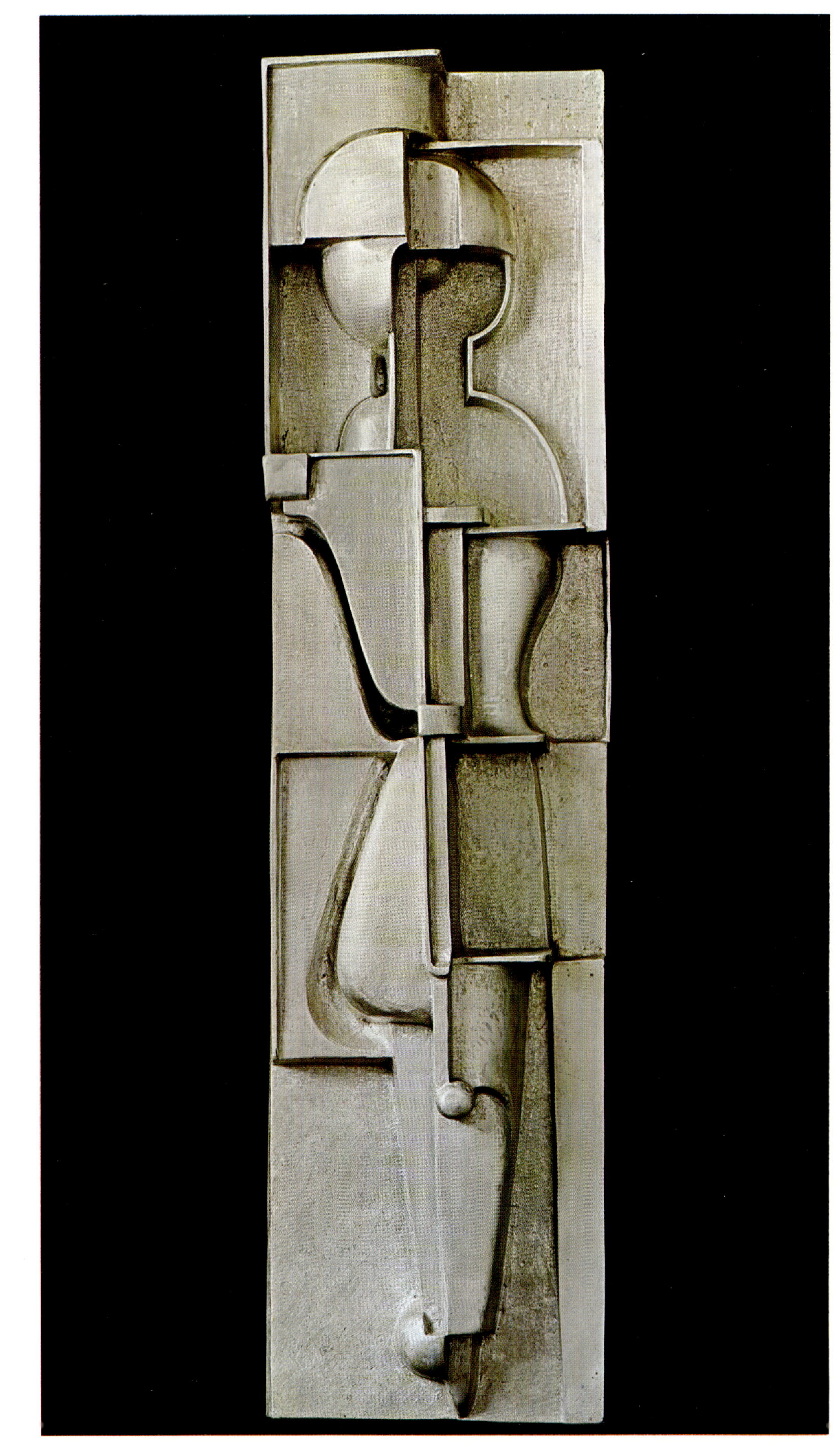

# Oskar Schlemmer

77 Ornamentalplastik
*(Ornamental Wall Sculpture)*
Silver, 1919
19 x 7¾″ (48.2 x 19.5 cm)
One of seven casts started in 1965

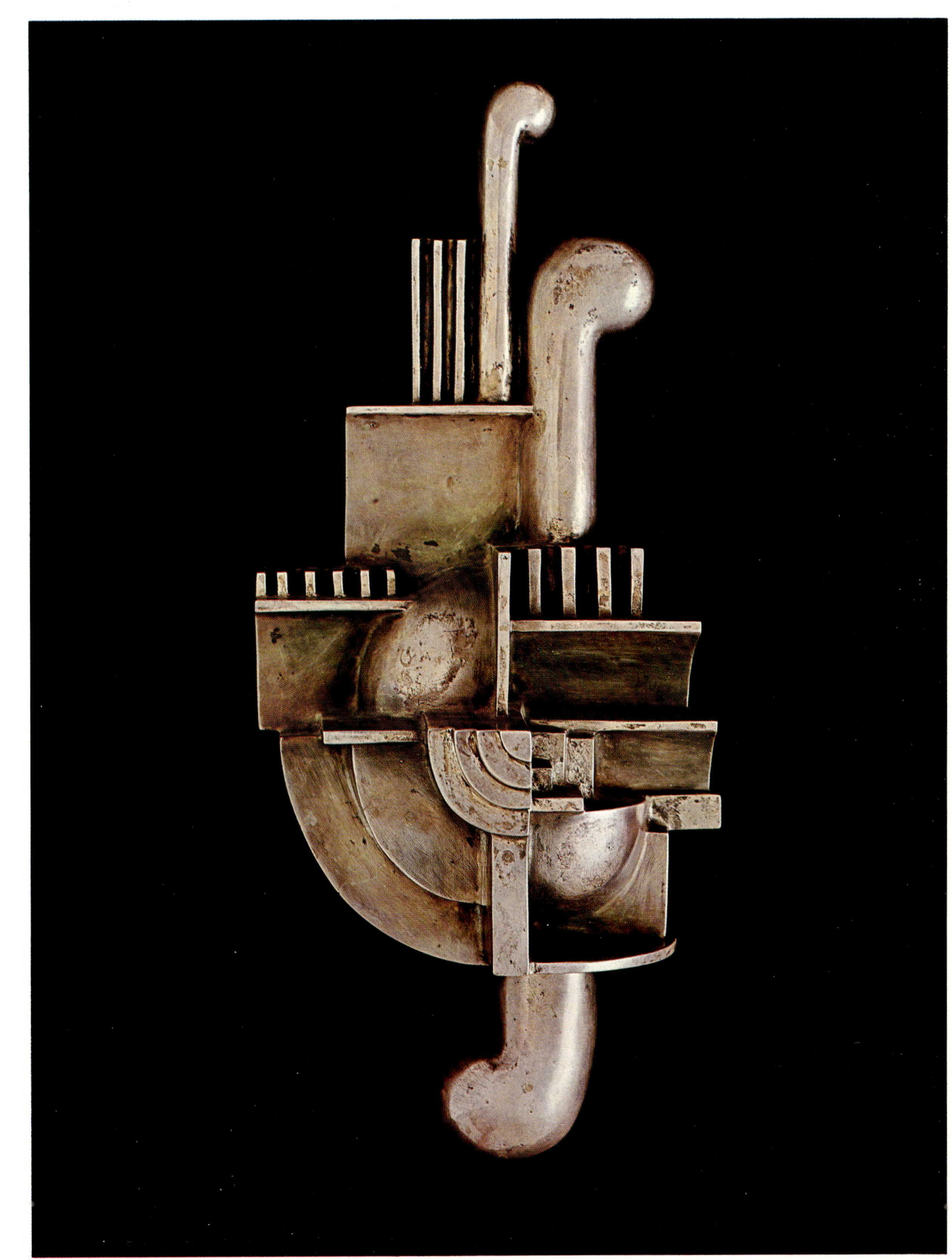

Oskar Schlemmer

**78** **Abstrakte Halbfigur im Profil nach Rechts**
*(Abstract Half-figure Profile Facing Right)*
Gouache, 1921
22⅛ x 16½″ (56.2 x 41.9 cm)
Signed lower right

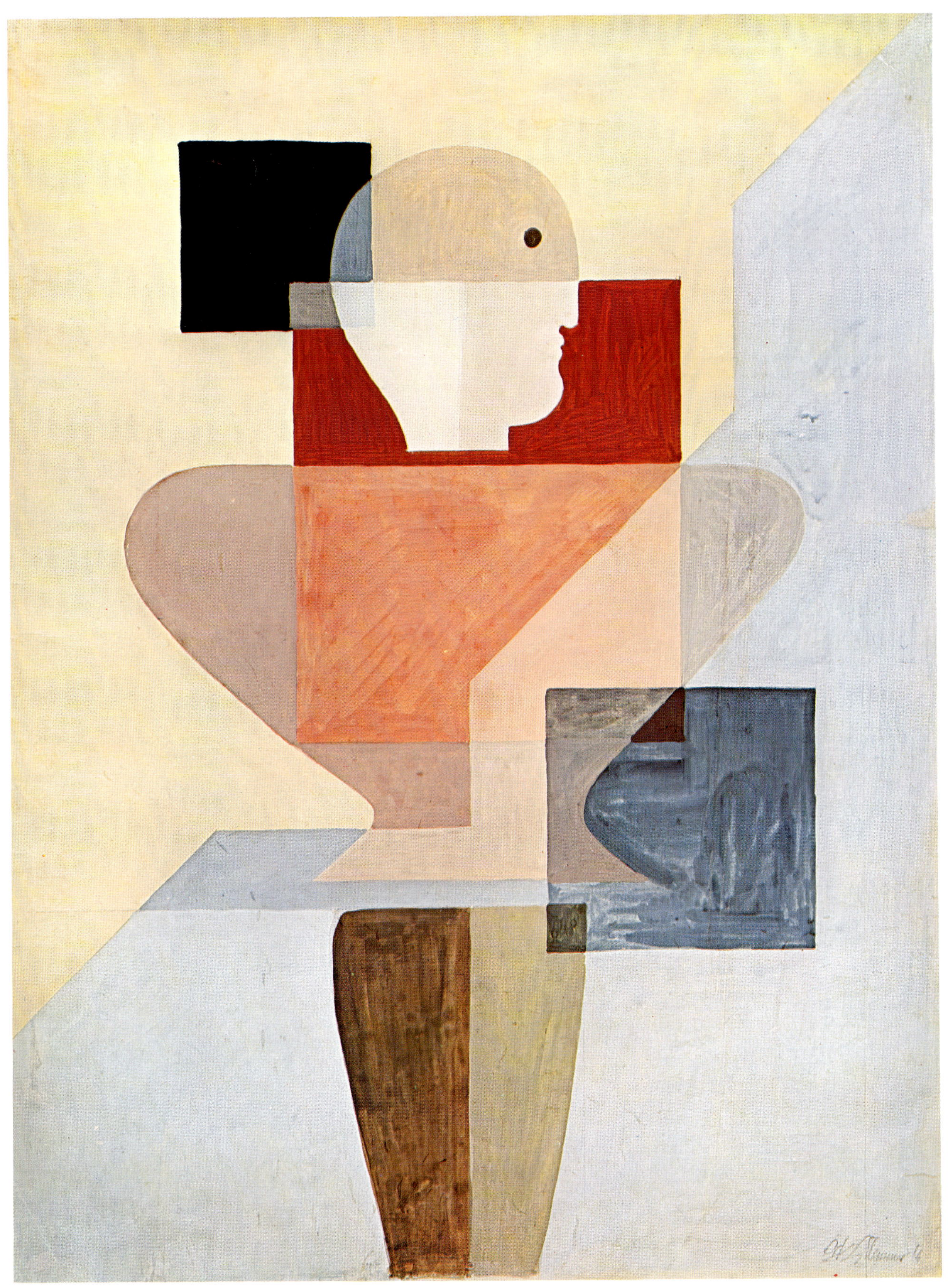

# Oskar Schlemmer

**79** **Profil nach links**
*(Profile Facing Left)*
Watercolor, pen and ink, 1925
10¼ x 8″ (26 x 20. 3 cm)
Dated lower right

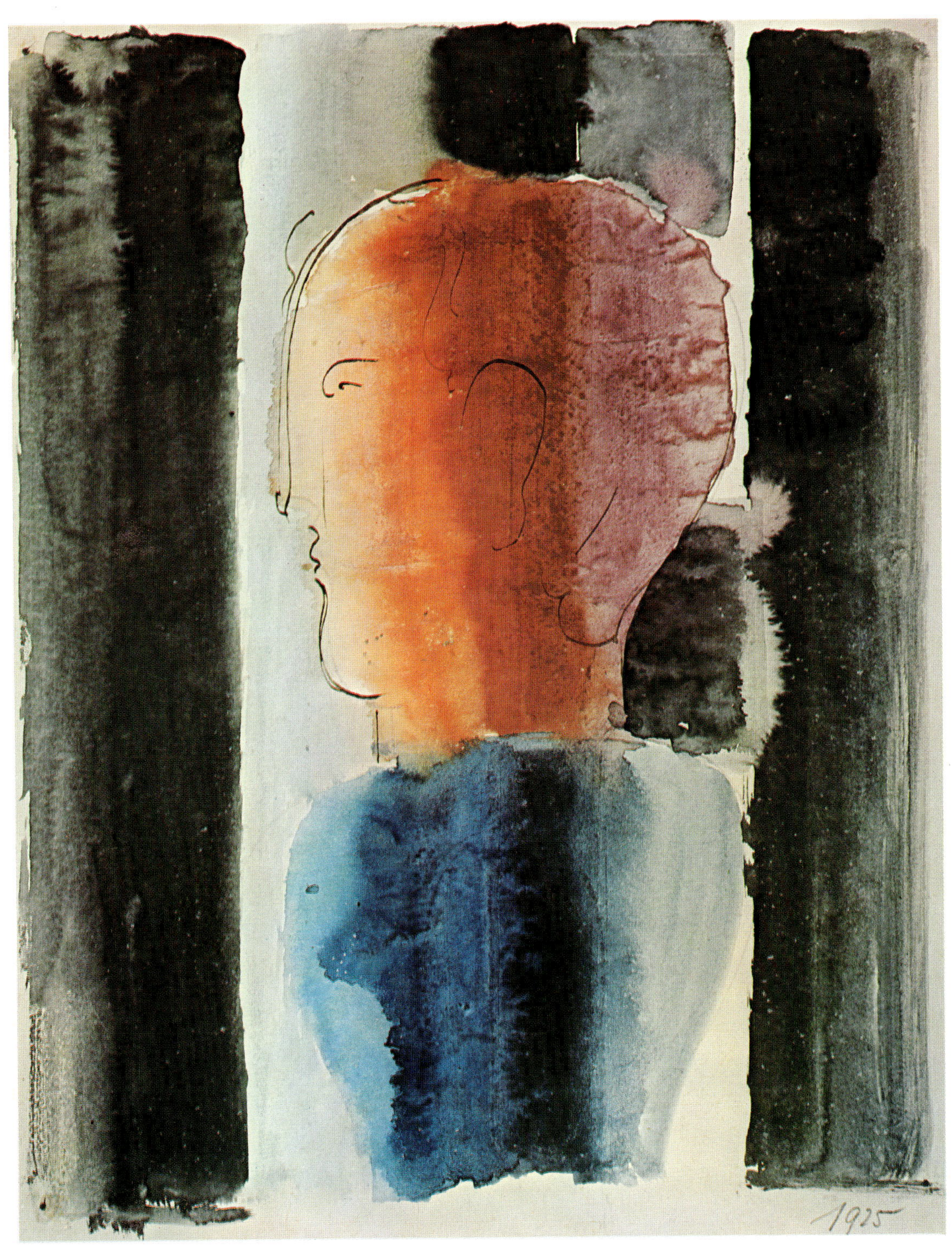

Oskar Schlemmer

80 Fünf Figuren vor Durchblick
*(Five Figures in a Vista)*
Watercolor, 1928
7⅛ x 9¼″ (18 x 23.5 cm)

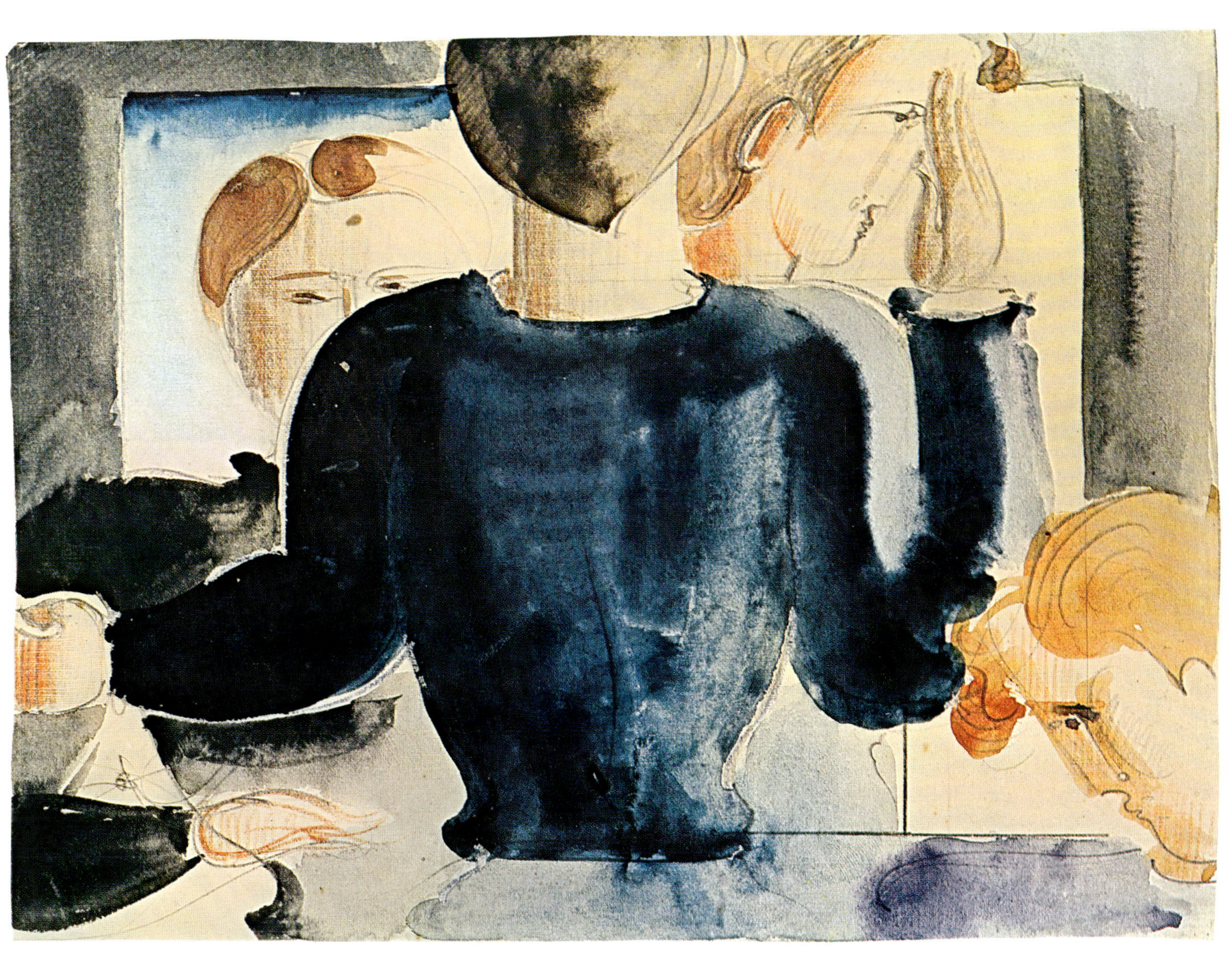

# Oskar Schlemmer

81 **Drahtfigur "Homo", Wandplastik**
*(Wire-Figure "Homo," Wall Sculpture)*
Steel wire on white painted wood, partly sprayed with black, 1931
151¾ x 100⅜" (285 x 255 cm)
One of an edition of ten started in 1968

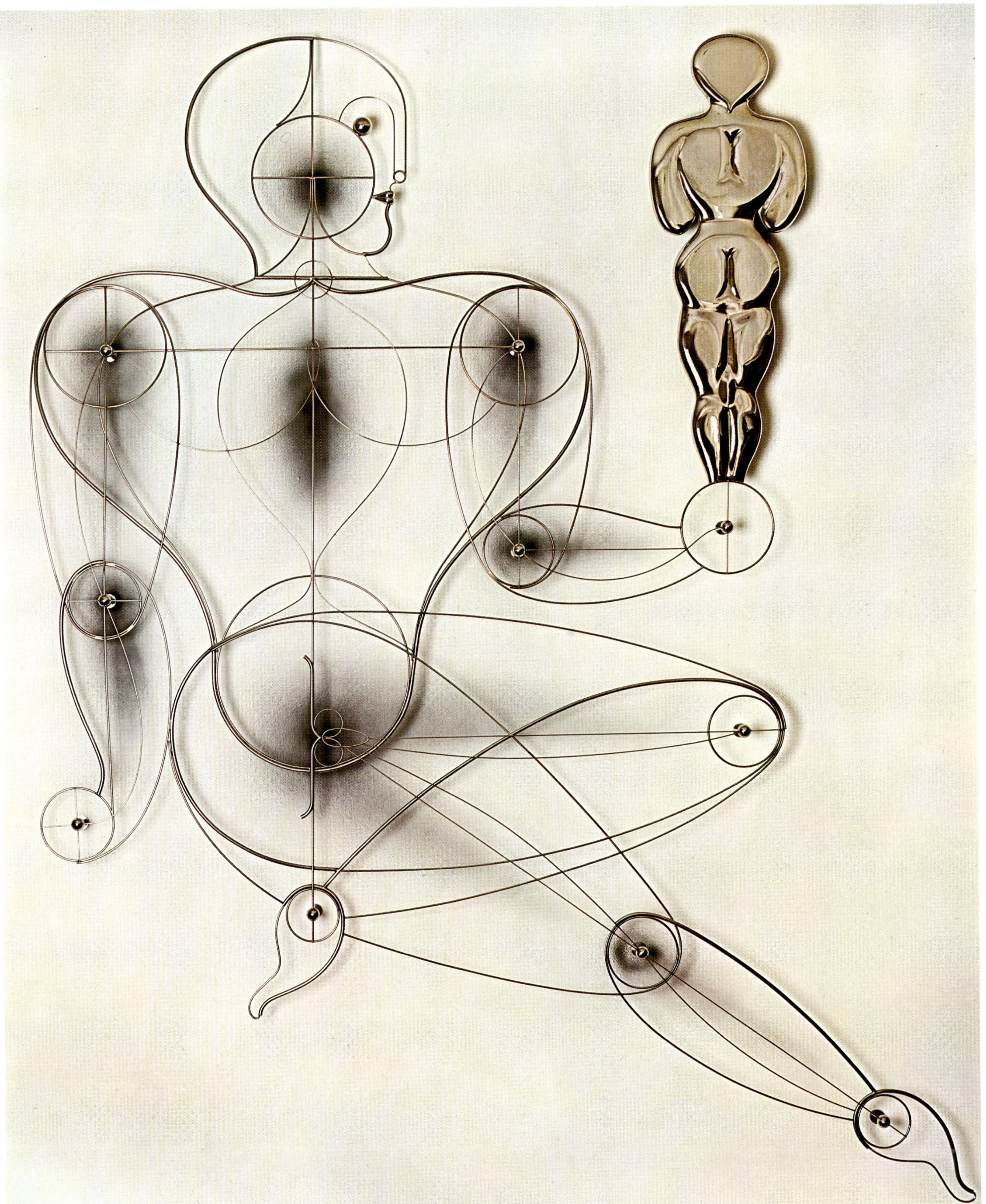

# Oskar Schlemmer



Kleiner Kopf, geneigt
*(Small Head, Inclined)*
Oil on grass cloth, on heavy cardboard, 1932
9 x 4⅝″ (23 x 11.7 cm)

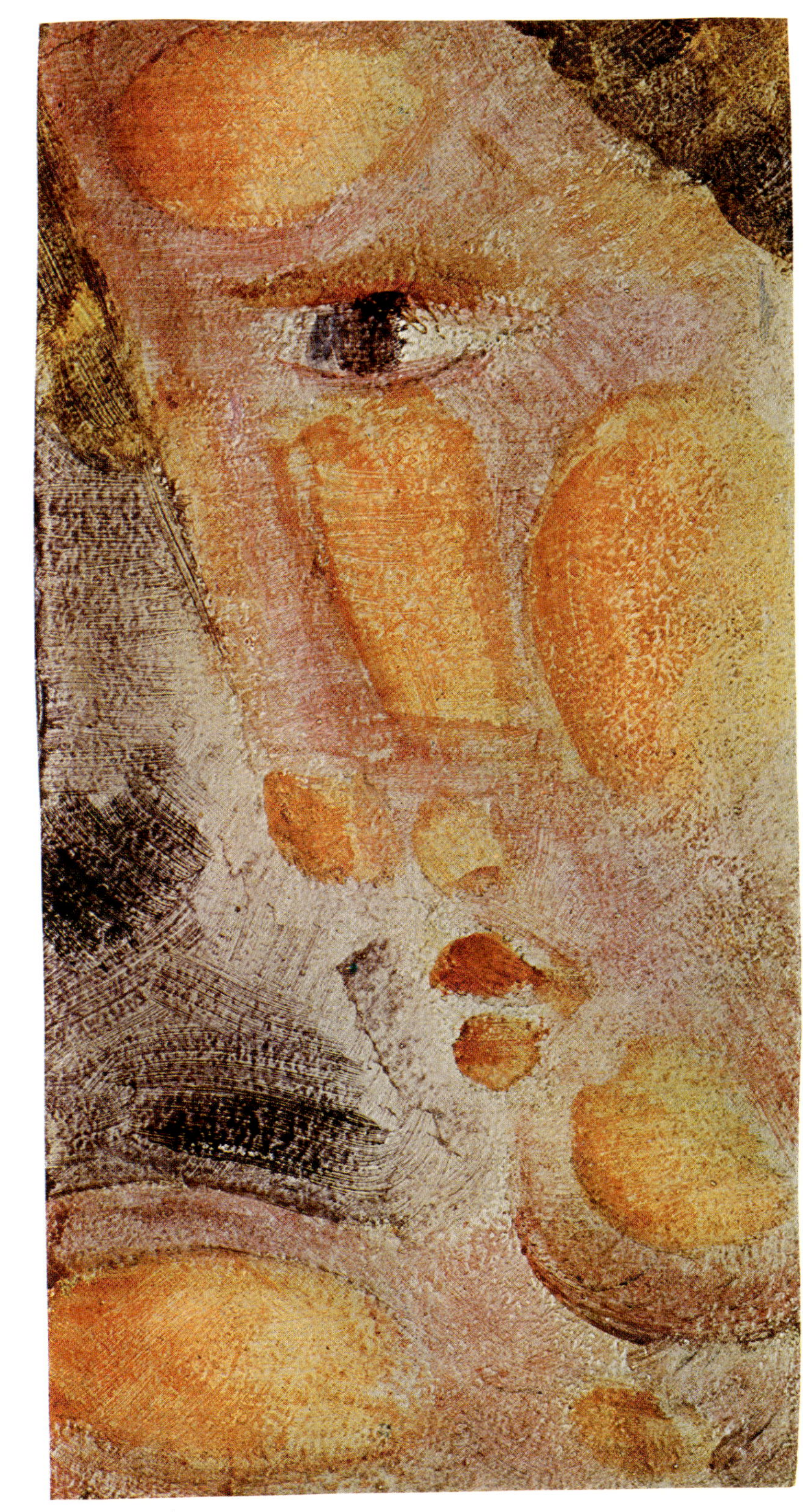

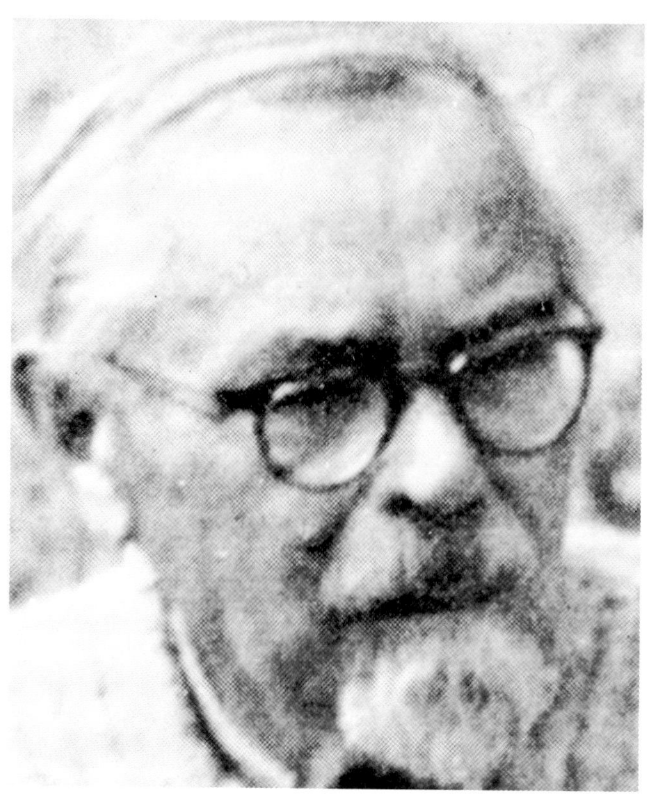

# Karl Schmidt-Rottluff

ROTTLUFF 1884 - LIVES IN BERLIN

83  Boats and Workmen
Watercolor, 1913
$12\frac{5}{8}$ x $16\frac{3}{4}''$ (32 x 42.5 cm)
Signed and dated lower left

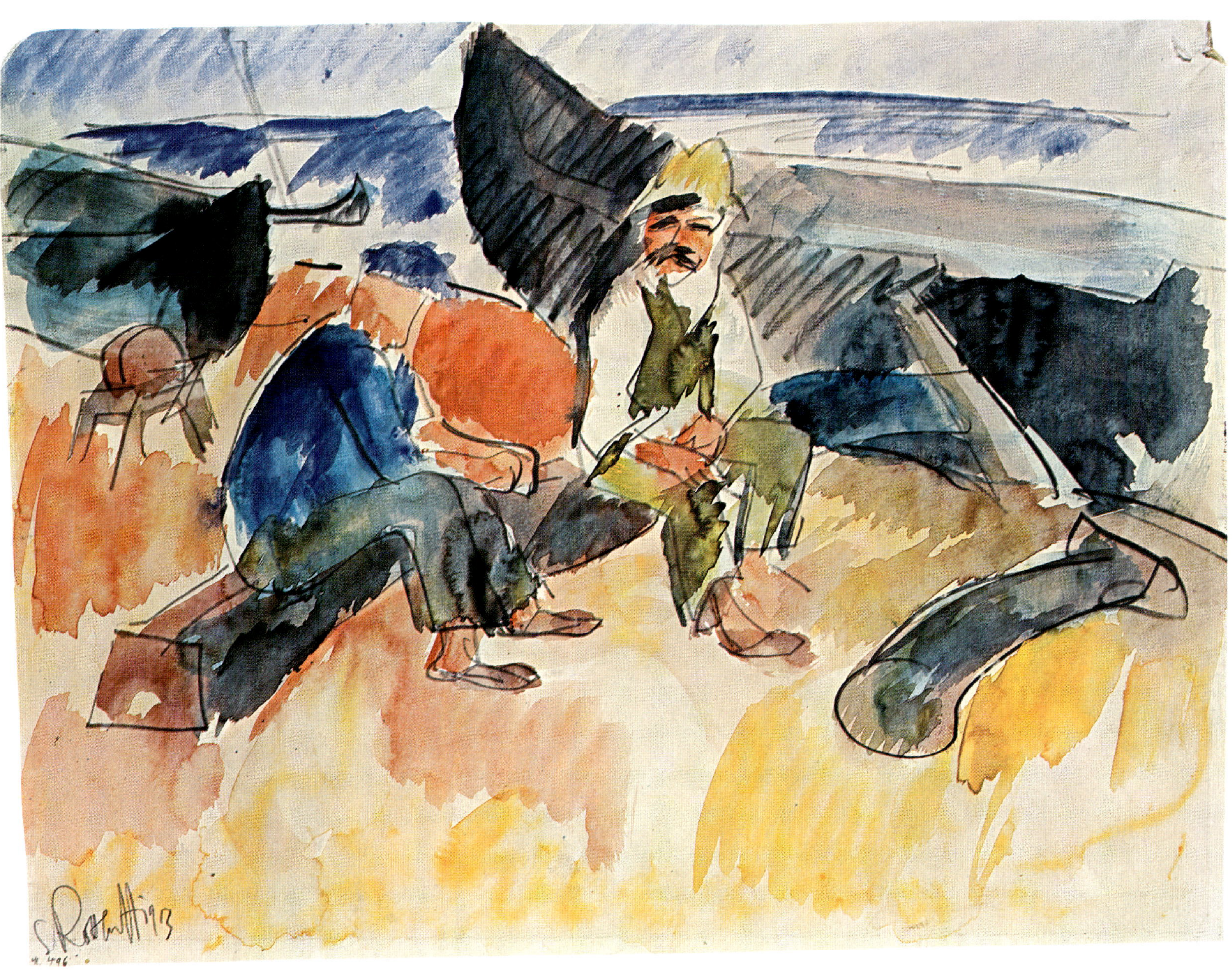

# Karl Schmidt-Rottluff

84 Two Schoolgirls
Oil on canvas, 1920
35½ x 29½″ (90 x 75 cm)
Signed lower right

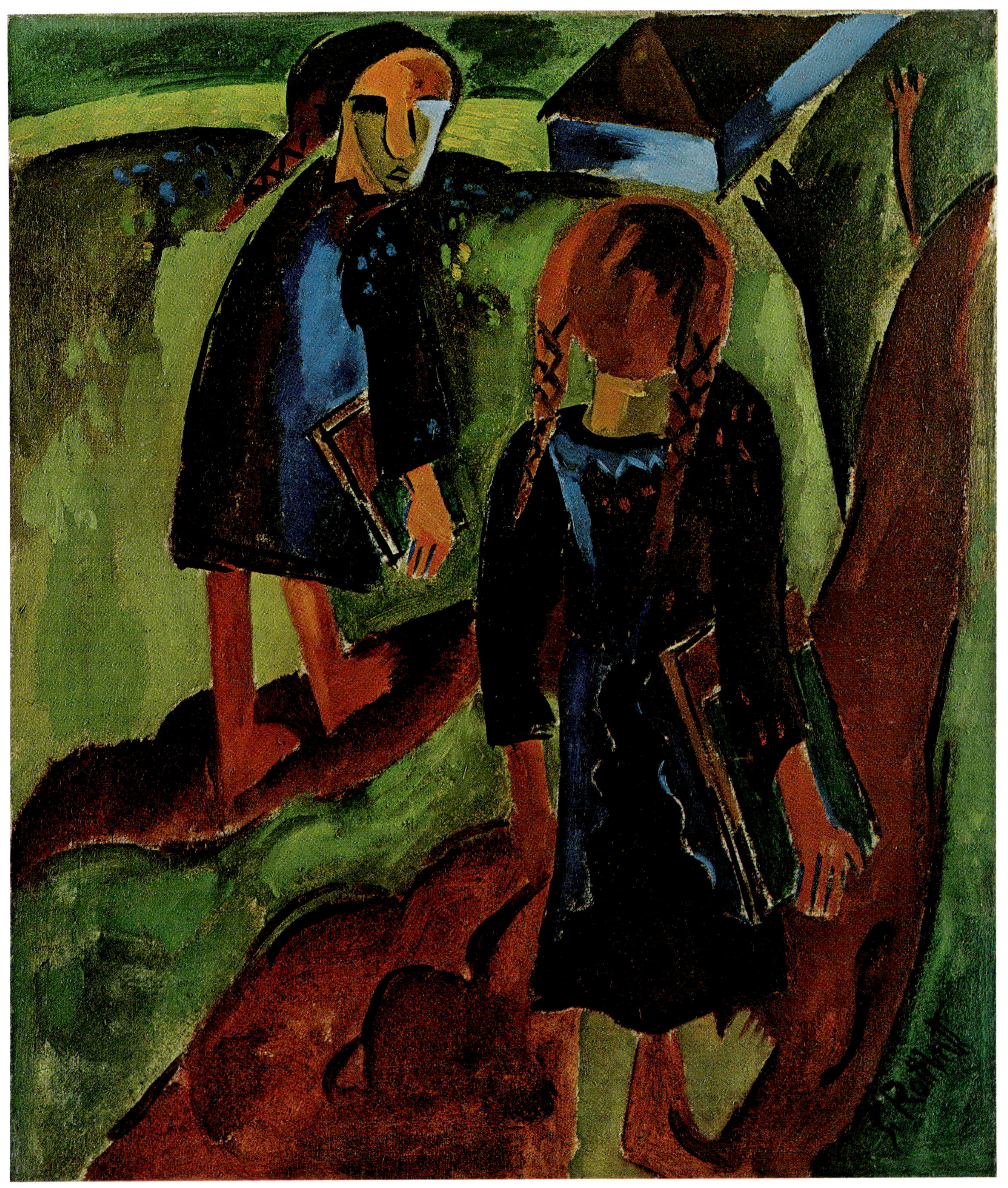

# Karl Schmidt-Rottluff

85 Waterlilies
Watercolor, 1934
$20\frac{1}{8} \times 27\frac{3}{8}''$ (51 x 69.5 cm)
Signed lower left

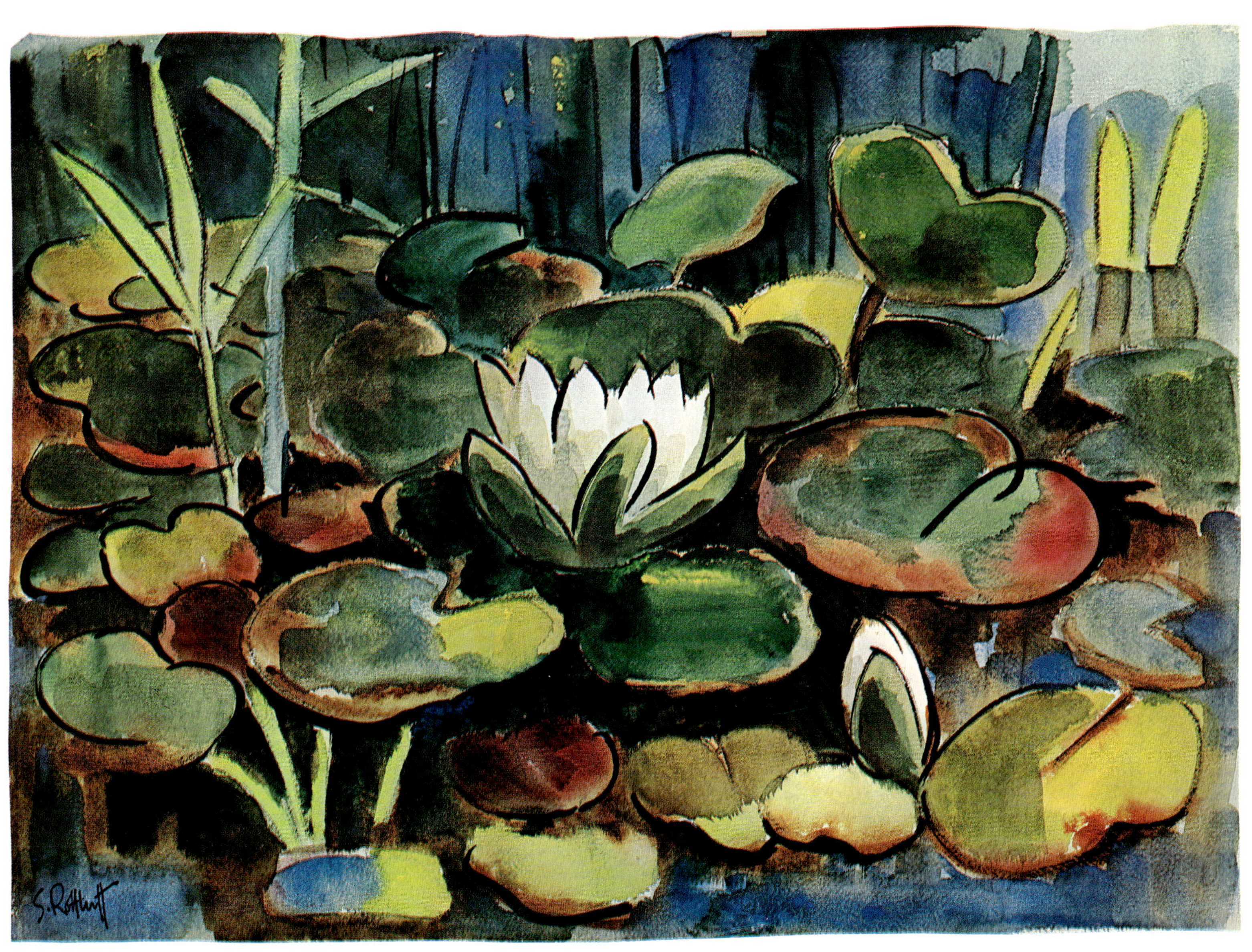

PHOTOGRAPHY: Robert E. Mates and Paul Katz
COLOR SEPARATIONS: Continental Color, New York
LITHOGRAPHY: Colorcraft Offset, New York
DESIGN: Andor Braun